California Natural History Guides: 36

NATIVE TREES
OF THE
SIERRA NEVADA

by
P. Victor Peterson and P. Victor Peterson, Jr.

Illustrated by
Rita Peterson, Barbara Thatcher, and Eugene Murman

California Natural History Guides
Arthur C. Smith, General Editor

Advisory Editorial Committee:
A. Starker Leopold
Robert Ornduff
Robert C. Stebbins

University of California Press
Berkeley and Los Angeles, California
University of California Press, Ltd.
London, England

ISBN: 0-520-02736-1 (clothbound)
       0-520-02666-7 (paperbound)
Library of Congress Catalog Card Number: 73-90671
Printed in the United States of America

CONTENTS

INTRODUCTION

Trees, like individuals, become increasingly more interesting as you become better acquainted with them. Traveling about California you will encounter an enormous number of different trees, which this book will help you identify.

On the high mountain trail there may be picturesque, wind-blown Western Junipers or the Limber Pines with long and droop-ing branches. A little farther down the trail the Lodgepole Pine, with its flaky bark, and the white-trunked Quaking Aspen. Still farther down the mountainside are the awe-inspiring Sierra Red-wood, the majestic Sugar Pine with long pendant cones hanging from the ends of its branches, the White Fir with erect cones glistening in the sunlight near the ends of its topmost branches, the Incense Cedar with its cinnamon-brown trunks, the lacy Douglas Fir, the Black Oak that was so important in the lives of the early Indians, and a host of other fascinating trees.

As you approach the dry foothills, the Digger Pine with its forked trunk, long gray-green needles, and big cones tells you that you have reached the lower limits of the conifers. On the valley floors below the rolling foothills, an entirely new group of trees appear, including the characteristic Valley Oak, the Fre-mont Cottonwood, and many other broadleaf trees. Near the desert the weird and grotesque Joshua Trees and the Yuccas begin to dot the landscape.

Along the central coast the sprawling, picturesque pines and cypresses of the Monterey Peninsula are silhouetted against the white sands and blue ocean, forming a series of never-to-be-forgotten vistas.

In California many areas have been set aside by the federal, state, or local governments to preserve for all time some of the beautiful and spectacular natural scenery with which the state is so abundantly blessed. Native trees are a major attraction in Torrey Pine State Park, Pfeiffer Big Sur State Park, Point Lobos

1

State Park, Anza-Borrego Desert State Park, Joshua Tree National Monument, Sequoia National Park, Kings Canyon National Park, Yosemite National Park, Redwood National Park, Inyo National Forest, Big Basin State Park, Muir Woods National Monument, and numerous state parks along the Redwood Highway from Armstrong Redwoods State Park near Santa Rosa to the Oregon border.

Three of the national parks referred to above lie within the scope of this book, and all include outstanding groves of Giant Sequoia (*Sequoiadendron giganteum*). One cannot stand in the shadow of the General Sherman Tree, the Lincoln Tree, the McKinley Tree, or the President Tree, or walk among those magnificent giants that constitute the Congress Group, all within Sequoia National Park, without experiencing a feeling of reverence for something so big and so old, yet still living. Some of these Giant Sequoias were large trees when Moses led the Israelites out of Egypt.

Equally impressive are the trees one sees after traveling across the Sierra Nevada, the Owens Valley, and into the White Mountains to an elevation of some 10,000 feet. Here on windswept and rock-strewn slopes are the Bristlecone Pines, now thought to be the oldest living things on this earth. They have been beautifully sculptured down through the ages by fire, windblown sand, and ice particles and appear almost like living driftwood. One wonders how they have been able to survive in this extreme environment for well over 4,000 years. Many of these short, squat monarchs were growing when the pyramids of Egypt were being built. While admiring them, one can ponder over the events of history that have taken place since the Methuselah Tree was a sapling 4,600 years ago.

California is truly a land of contrasts. This is largely because of its size and topography. It covers an area of 158,693 square miles and extends 600 miles in a true north-south direction. Elevations vary from -282 to 14,494 feet. These conditions and the fact that the entire western boundary of the state is the Pacific Ocean mainly account for the wide climatic variation. Since the natural distribution of native plants is largely influenced

2

by climatic and soil conditions, it is readily understandable why there are so many different native plants, including trees, to be found in California. Many native animals, likewise, tend to seek areas which are climatically satisfactory for their survival.

Because trees are stationary and usually more conspicuous than other plants or animals they serve in general as indicators of plant distribution.

The Sierra Nevada and environs, which include national parks, forests, monuments, and state parks, provide not only an excellent place to study native trees but also a spectacular vacation locale. Many of these areas provide a wide variety of wholesome recreational activities, including camping, hiking, horseback riding, fishing, and hunting during the appropriate seasons.

It is our hope that the tree trails suggested here will entice you into this fascinating country and help you get acquainted not only with the trees of the Sierra Nevada but the entire flora and fauna. When you visit the Sierra Nevada, don't neglect its physiographic and geological features. Here are just a few to whet your appetite: Stand on Glacier Point in Yosemite National Park and gaze at the canyons below with their precipitous granite walls and magnificent waterfalls and the rocky peaks beyond. Before you leave the Glacier Point area visit the lone Jeffrey Pine growing out of solid rock on the barren top of Sentinel Dome. The growth and survival of this grand tree is a real mystery. As you approach the valley, stop after passing through the Wawona Tunnel and take another look at the valley from that point. Stop at Visitor's Center on the floor of the valley for an explanation of the geological formation of the valley. Drive the winding road to the Kings Canyon National Park and read the geological history revealed in its perpendicular walls. Climb Moro Rock in Sequoia National Park and look beyond to the Kaweah Peaks and the Great Western Divide. Stand on the shores of Lake George in the Mammoth Lakes area, with Crystal Crag in the foreground, a view long to be remembered. On the road to the Devil's Post Pile National Monument, stop at Mammoth Earthquake Fault, walk between its perpendicular walls on a snow patch that persists even in midsummer. Don't miss the stop at Minaret Summit with Branner Peak and Mt. Ritter in the foreground; here you will find a White Bark Pine nearby. Scores of spectacular vistas exist in the Lake Tahoe area including Desolation Valley. These are but a few of the thrills that await you when you visit the Sierra Nevada, if you take time to enjoy its beauty and grandeur.

Make it a habit as you travel the highways and byways of California or as you camp on the banks of some stream or lake or in the shadow of the mountains, to become better acquainted with the beautiful native trees — you will find it rewarding. This book has been prepared as a guide to aid in the recognition of the trees of the Sierra Nevada, for only as you know them by name can you think or talk about them.

The Sierra Nevada, for the purpose of this book, encompasses the whole range including the entire eastern and western slopes; also included in this book are the White, Inyo and Panamint mountains to the east. For native trees in other areas in California, see *Native Trees of the San Francisco Region* by Woodbridge Metcalf (Berkeley and Los Angeles, 1959), and *Native Trees of Southern California*, by P. Victor Peterson (Berkeley and Los Angeles, 1970).

Only native or naturalized trees are treated in this book. To identify any of the hundreds of introduced species, a person should consult one of the more extensive publications dealing with cultivated trees. Nursery catalogs, nurserymen, teachers of botany or forestry, landscape designers, or the owners of particular trees may prove helpful in identifying an individual specimen. Many ornamental trees are either of foreign origin or may be the product of careful and scientific hybridizing. Often the common names applied to these non-native hybridized trees bear no relationship to the names of their ancestors. Even though the great majority of our street and park trees are non-native, the charm and beauty of many of our native trees should not be overlooked when planning home or community grounds.

Most of the black and white species illustrations were made specifically for this book by Rita Whitmore Peterson. However, Dusky Willow and McKenzie Willow were made available by Stanford University Press from Leroy Abrams, *Illustrated Flora of the Pacific*

States. Drawings of Arizona Ash, Hinds Black Walnut and Parry Manzanita, Miners Dogwood, Mountain Mahogany, Lombardy Poplar, Silver Poplar, Sierra Plum, and Tree of Heaven were taken from University of California Press books by Woodbridge Metcalf, Willis Jepson, Howard McMinn, and Evelyn Maino. The maps were drawn by Barbara J. Thatcher. The water color drawings are by Eugene Murman. The authors wish to express their appreciation to the Department of Special Collections, University Research Library, University of California at Los Angeles, for permission to reproduce in reduced form these outstanding drawings which are part of a special collection of that library.

WHAT IS A TREE?

A tree, as defined in this book, is a woody plant at least 10 feet high with a distinct stem or trunk not less than 2 inches in diameter and, except for unbranched yuccas or palms, with a more or less well-defined crown. Among the willows, oaks, maples, dogwoods, manzanitas, and others, there are certain species which do not usually attain tree dimensions; these are classified as shrubs and will not be treated in this book. It is rather difficult to describe specifically the physical characteristics of all members even of a single species. The growth pattern of an individual specimen will, in many cases, depend markedly upon the surrounding conditions. Frequently certain oaks or willows appear quite shrubby, while other members of the same species growing under ideal conditions develop into definitely tree like specimens, Caution must be exercised in comparing the size, shape, and characteristics of an individual leaf with the accepted standard. Averages should always be used when making comparisons. Fruit characteristics usually show less variation than leaves. Bark characteristics are inconclusive. However, as one becomes familiar with the general characteristics — leaves, fruit, bark, and silhouette — the identification of individual species becomes less difficult and the effort more gratifying.

Leaves of trees may be classified as broad or narrow. Leaves that are generally 3/16 inch wide or less are, in this book, classed as narrow leaves. They may be needle-shaped (pines), linear (firs), or scale-shaped (cypresses). California trees with such leaves are all evergreen since they retain their leaves for more than one season. Leaves that are generally more than 3/16 inch wide are classed as broad leaves. They may be either simple or compound, may have margins which are smooth, toothed, serrated, or lobed, and may be arranged opposite each other or alternately along the stem. Trees with broad leaves may be either deciduous or evergreen.

6

A TREE IS A PLANT

with a trunk or stem

that is

woody

10 or more
feet high

2 or more inches
in diameter

and has a crown

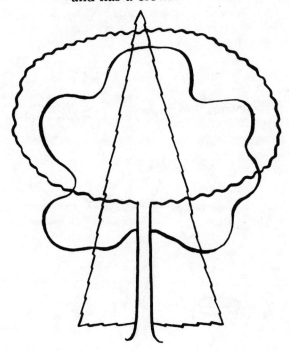

A TREE HAS

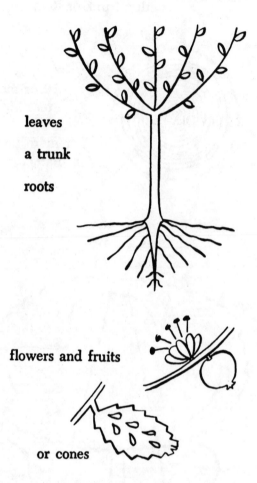

leaves

a trunk

roots

flowers and fruits

or cones

that produce seeds

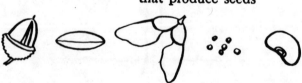

LEAVES

ARE ON EVERGREEN TREES

spring   summer   fall   winter

OR ON DECIDUOUS TREES

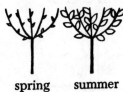

spring   summer   fall   winter

ARE NARROW   ¼″ or less wide

OR BROAD   more than ¼″ wide

oval   oblong   ovate   elliptical   linear

cordate   deltoid   obovate   oblanceolate

lanceolate

LEAVES

ARE SIMPLE OR COMPOUND

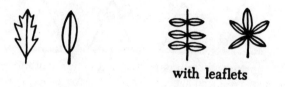

with leaflets

ARE OPPOSITE OR ALTERNATE

Pinnate, bipinnate, tripinnate, or palmate

HAVE MARGINS THAT ARE

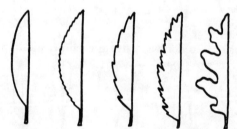

smooth   serrate   toothed   doubly   lobed
                                toothed

HOW TO IDENTIFY TREES

There are many features which contribute to the recognition of a particular species of tree, such as leaves, flowers, fruit, bark, size, silhouette, and habitat. However, leaves probably offer the best initial clue, since they are usually distinctive and in most cases may be found on the tree or the ground nearby. With this thought in mind, the following simple key has been prepared. In some cases the key leads directly to a specific tree, in other cases to groups of related trees. When the tree or group has been identified with the aid of the key, turn to the description in the text and to the illustration for further and final verification. If you have not used identification keys before see the sections on the use of natural history keys in Jaeger and Smith, *Introduction to the Natural History of Southern California* (Berkeley and Los Angeles, 1966) and Smith, *Introduction to the Natural History of the San Francisco Bay Region* (Berkeley and Los Angeles, 1959). See the glossary for definitions of scientific words used in key.

Key to Trees of Sierra Nevada

1. Leaves generally less than 3/16 inch wide.

    2. Leaves needle-shaped and arranged in bundles of 1 to 5, wrapped at base with sheath of papery scales . . . Pines, p. 33

    2. Leaves not needle-shaped and not arranged in bundles.

        3. Leaves linear, typically 1/2 to 2 1/2 inches long.

            4. Leaves sharp-pointed, appear 2-ranked because of twist at base. Fruit not a cone.

                5. Fruit green, drupelike . . . California Nutmeg, p. 52

                5. Fruit red, berrylike, cup-shaped   Western Yew, p. 52

            4. Leaves blunt, not sharp-pointed, fruit a cone.

5. Leaves usually less than 1 inch long and joined to tiny woody pegs. Cones 1 to 3 inches long, bracts not extending beyond cone scales . . . . Mountain Hemlock, p. 43

5. Leaves 1 inch long, not joined to woody pegs.

    6. Leaf scars slightly raised. Cones 2 to 4 inches long, pendant. Conspicuous 3-pointed bracts protruding between cone scales . . . . Douglas Fir, p. 42

    6. Leaf scars not raised, cones erect on upper branches.

        7. Leaves somewhat flattened, constricted and twisted near base causing leaves to appear 2-ranked . . . . . . White Fir, p. 44

        7. Leaves not somewhat flattened, or constricted, or twisted at base. Sometimes curved upward around twig . . Red Fir, p. 45

3. Leaves scale-shaped.

    4. Leaves closely appressed, only tips free, 4-ranked, 2 outer rows keel-shaped and overlapping 2 inner rows, leaf-bearing twigs flattened. Cones 3/4 to 1 inch long consisting of 2 large scales separated from a closed center of 2 to 4 sharp-pointed scales. . . . . Incense Cedar, p. 47

    4. Leaves closely overlapping, with dorsal glands, 4-ranked. Cones 3/4 to 1 1/4 inch long more or less spherical. Scales shield-shaped, apex with prominent central hump or prickle . . . . . Cypress, p. 48

    4. Leaves closely overlapping, attached in circles of 3, with or without glands. Cones berrylike, 1/4 to 1/3 inch long, globular, bluish black with white bloom when mature . . . . Junipers, p. 49

3. Leaves awl-shaped, 1/8 to 1/2 inch long, partially overlapping each other, pointed tips spreading out more or less from twig. Cone 2 to 3 inches long, thick woody scales . . . . Giant Sequoia, p. 46

12

1. Leaves usually more than 3/16 inches wide.

    2. Leaves long, narrow, and stiff.

        3. Leaves 6 to 10 inches long, 2 inches or less wide at base, sharp-pointed . . . . Joshua Tree, p.53

        3. Leaves 18 to 36 inches long, 2 to 3 inches wide at base, sharp-pointed . . . . Mojave Yucca, p.54

    2. Leaves not long, or narrow, or stiff.

        3. Plants evergreen, leaves persistent.

            4. Leaves simple, not lobed.

                5. Fruit an acorn . . . . Evergreen Oaks, p. 71
                                       Tanbark Oak, p. 67

                5. Fruit an olive-green drupe, purple when ripe, flowers yellowish, in umbels, leaves 3 to 5 inches long, oblong lanceolate or lanceolate, smooth, thick, entire, odorous when crushed . . . . California Laurel, p. 72

                5. Fruit an achene with long hairy tail, flowers solitary or in small clusters, leaves small, 1/2 to 1 1/2 inches long . . . . Mountain Mahogany and Hard Tack, p. 74,75

                5. Fruit a bur, chestnutlike, almost enclosing a shiny, light brown nut . . . . . . Chinquapin, p. 67

                5. Fruit, berrylike, in clusters, orange to red or reddish brown when ripe.

                    6. Small tree or shrub, leaves 2 to 4 inches long, margin serrate . . . . Toyon, p. 79

                    6. Medium to large tree, 30 ft to 100 ft, smooth terra-cotta bark, leaves 3 to 6 inches long, margins entire . . . . Madrone, p. 90

                    6. Shrub or small tree to 22 ft; smooth red or chocolate colored bark, leaves 1 to 1 1/2 inches long, margins entire . . . . Parry or Common Manzanita, p. 91

            4. Leaves simple, lobed.

5. Fruit an acorn. Leaves with sharp, shallow, forward-pointing lobes tipped with a spine
. . . . Oracle Oak, p. 72

5. Fruit an ovoid capsule, 1 1/2 to 2 1/2 inches in diameter. Leaves 1 to 3 inches long, 1/2 to 2 inches wide, larger on shoots, 3- to 5-lobed, rarely entire, usually 3-veined from base, flowers large and showy, yellow or orange
. . . . California Flannel Bush, p. 82

3. Leaves deciduous.

4. Leaves simple, not lobed.

5. Fruit in pods 1 1/2 to 3 inches long, dull red when ripe. Leaves 2 to 3 1/2 inches in diameter almost round, heart-shaped at base. Flowers showy, deep reddish pink to reddish purple appear before leaves. . . . . Western Redbud, p. 80

5. Fruit a samara. Leaves 1 to 2 inches long, 1 to 2 inches wide, broadly ovate, almost round, entire or slightly rounded serrate, usually single, sometimes compound with 2 or 3 leaflets. Flowers greenish, without petals . . . . . . Dwarf Ash, p. 95

5. Fruit a drupe with bony pit, usually containing a single seed.

6. Leaves 1 to 2 inches long, 1/2 to 1 inch wide, eliptic to roundish, finely serrate alternate. *No glands at base of leaf or on leaf stalk.* Flowers in short clusters of 2 to 4, fruit red to yellowish when ripe . . . . Sierra Plum, p. 78

6. Leaves 3/4 to 3 1/2 inches long, 1/2 to 1 3/4 inches wide, finely serrate, alternate, *tiny glands at base of leaf or on leaf stalk near base of leaf.* Flower in racemes or short clusters, fruit dark red to purple when ripe . . . Cherries, p. 76

5. Fruit a berrylike drupe with 2 to 4 separate nutlets.

6. Leaves alternate, 2 1/2 to 8 inches long, flowers greenish-white in umbels. Fruit black, spherical, 1/4 to 1/2 inch in diameter. Shrub or small tree to 20 ft . . . . Cascara Sagrada, p. 87

6. Leaves opposite, fruit 2-celled with 2-seeded stone.

7. Fruit purple-black and shining when ripe.
Shrub or small tree to 15 ft
. . . . Miners Dogwood, p. 89

7. Fruit bright red, Shrub or tree to 40 ft
. . . . Mountain Dogwood, p. 89

5. Fruit, small woody cones. Flowers in catkins.

6. Cones solitary, 7/8 to 1 inch long, disintegrates
on tree. Leaves 1 1/2 to 2 1/2 inches long, more
than 1/2 as wide, sharply serrate, parallel side
veins . . . . Water Birch, p. 64

6. Cones in clusters, drop as entire cones. Leaves
2 to 4 inches long, 1 1/2 to 2 1/2 inches wide
straight, parallel side veins . . . . . Alders, p. 65

5. Fruit a capsule 2- to 4-valved with many seeds.
Flowers in catkins.

6. Leaf blades at least 4 times as long as wide,
buds covered with only 1 scale . . . Willows, p. 59

6. Leaves 1 to 3 1/2 inches long, broadly ovate
pointed at apex, *leaf stalk flattened,* side
veins irregularly branched
. . . . . Aspen and Fremont Cottonwood, p. 57

6. Leaves 2 1/2 to 5 inches long, 2 to 3 inches wide,
broadest near base pointed towards apex, leaf
stalk, round and stout. . Black Cottonwood, p. 58

4. Leaves, simple lobed.

5. Fruit an acorn . . . . Deciduous Oaks, p. 69

5. Fruit a double samara.

6. Leaves 3/4 to 1 1/2 inches long, 3/4 to 2 inches
wide, palmately 3-lobed
. . . . Mountain Maple, p. 83,84

6. Leaves 6 to 18 inches long and as wide, 3- to
5-lobed, lobes may be 2- to 4-toothed or
almost entire . . . . Big Leaf Maple, p. 85

15

5. Fruit a small nutlet in bristly "button-balls" 3/4
   to 1 inch in diameter. Leaves 5 to 10 inches long,
   6 to 12 inches wide, 3- to 5-lobed. Conspicuous
   stipules at base of petioles . Western Sycamore, p. 73

4. Leaves pinnately compound.

   5. Fruit a double samara. Leaflets 3 or 5, rarely 7
      or 9, each leaflet more or less lobed or deeply
      serrate . . . . Box Elder, p. 86

   5. Fruit a samara, usually 1-seeded with terminal
      wing.

      6. Leaves, 3 to 9 leaflets, usually finely serrate
         above middle . . . . Ashes, p. 93

      6. Leaves, 11 to 31 leaflets, 3 to 5 inches long,
         1 to 2 inches wide, entire except for 1 to 4
         blunt glandular teeth near base
         . . . . Tree of Heaven, p. 80

   5. Fruit a small spherical berrylike drupe. Leaves,
      5 to 9 leaflets, 1 to 4 inches long, sessile or very
      short stalked. Flowers small, white in flat-topped
      clusters. Fruit dark blue with whitish bloom
      . . . . Blue Elderberry, p. 97

   5. Fruit a spherical, thick-shelled, shallow-grooved
      nut enclosed in a green, pulpy husk
      . . . . Hinds Black Walnut, p. 63

4. Leaves palmately compound. Fruit a pearlike pod.
   Leaves, 5 to 7 leaflets, oblong lanceolate serrate.
   Flowers pinkish-white with orange anthers in long
   erect cylindrical clusters, 6 to 10 inches long
   . . . . California Buckeye, p. 88

To distinguish between certain species of the same genus, one will
frequently need to compare other features in addition to leaves,
such as flowers, fruit, bark characteristics, size, silhouette, and
habitat. The height indicated for each species applies to the mature
tree in its natural habitat unless otherwise indicated. The months
listed in the species descriptions following the descriptions of
leaves, flowers, and fruit refer to the average flowering period of
that species when it is found in its natural habitat.

RECOGNIZING TREES AT A DISTANCE

After you become expert at identifying trees close up you may wish to develop your skill recognizing them from afar. In most cases certain characteristics of the silhouette are sufficiently distinctive so that with practice the species may be identified as you drive by in your car. Verification by hiking over for a close look at the leaves will enable you to fix in mind the characteristics to watch for the next time you see the tree in question. To assist you in learning to recognize trees from a distance, some of the common trees are illustrated in silhouette and their characteristics are discussed. More and more California native trees are being planted in parks, along city streets and in gardens of homes far from their native habitat. Under these conditions tree silhouettes may vary somewhat from those found in nature.

The Sugar Pine (*Pinus lambertiana*) is readily recognized by its long, pendulous cones which hang from near the ends of the characteristic horizontal branches.

The Digger Pine (*Pinus sabiniana*) is most readily recognized by its long, gray-green needles, large cones, and forked trunk. It must not be confused with the Coulter Pine (*Pinus coulteri*), which also produces large heavy cones, but has a straight trunk and dark green foliage resembling somewhat the foliage of the Jeffrey Pine.

Western Yellow Pine (*Pinus ponderosa*) is abundant in the main timber belt of the entire Sierra Nevada. Mature trees are tall and straight with massive trunks that are frequently free of branches for a considerable distance. Young trees in open stands will have branches beginning near the ground. Bark of mature tree is a tawny yellow to russet brown, broken into shieldlike platelets. Bark of young trees or trees growing in a less favorable environment is a dark reddish brown or blackish and narrowly furrowed. A near relative, the Jeffrey Pine (*Pinus jeffreyi*) is frequently confused with the Western Yellow Pine. However, there are definable differences in cones, silhouette, bark and habitat which will be revealed by comparative studies in the field.

Douglas
Fir

Ponderosa
Pine

Incense
Cedar

Black
Oak

Mountain
Dogwood

Black
Cottonwood

Sugar
Pine

Jeffrey   Lodgepole   Mackenzie   Mountain
 Pine   Pine   Willow   Alder

White	White	Quaking	Red
Fir	Fir	Aspen	Fir
(young)	(mature)		

The One-Leaf Pinon Pine (*Pinus monophylla*) is the only one-needle native pine. Young trees are quite pyramidal, but with age the lower branches die and the upper branches tend to spread, producing a somewhat more irregular and open crown. It is found primarily on dry slopes and frequently with the California Juniper (*Juniperus californica*).

The young White Fir (*Abies concolor*) is a beautiful pyramidal tree; with age the crown tends to become roundish. Many old trees have dead and irregular tops. Cones of all firs stand erect on the topmost branches and disintegrate on the tree. Cones of the White Fir are somewhat smaller than those of the Red Fir (*Abies magnifica*).

The young Red Fir (*Abies magnifica*) like the young White Fir is a beautiful pyramidal tree, which tends to age in somewhat the same fashion as does the White Fir. However, there are some characteristic differences. Bark on the mature Red Fir is a deep dark reddish brown while that of the White Fir is a rough ashen gray. Top branches of the Red Fir are somewhat stiffer than those of the White Fir. Foliage of the Red Fir is a dark blue green while that of the White Fir is a more dull green. In order to firmly fix in mind the readily identifiable differences between these two closely related species, locate side-by-side examples of each and compare their differences and similarities.

The young Incense Cedar (*Calocedrus decurrens*) is another beautiful pyramidal tree. Crowns of the older trees tend to become open and irregular. The flattened leaf-bearing twigs which lie primarily in one plane tend to give the tree a somewhat lacy appearance. Its trunk and thick fibrous cinnamon-brown bark resemble somewhat the trunk and bark of the Giant Sequoia (*Sequoiadendron giganteum*).

A mature Western Juniper (*Juniperus occidentalis*), so picturesque in the high mountains, is readily recognized by its usually gnarled form, short, stocky, weather-beaten, cinnamon-brown tapering trunk, and its flat top and open crown. However, in a more favorable environment, it frequently develops a straight and less tapering trunk and a somewhat pyramidal crown. The bark on more protected trees is usually less fluted and not as deeply colored as that of the older trees found in a more severe environment.

22

Giant Sequoia (*S. giganteum*) is by all odds the most imposing tree of the Sierra Nevada. The mature trees are readily recognized by their massive columnar and strongly buttressed trunks and by the distinctive orange-tan to cinnamon-red color of their thick fibrous bark. The young trees have a distinctive pyramidal crown which becomes rounded and frequently broken as the tree matures. A mature tree consists essentially of a central trunk without branches for a long way and an irregular crown composed primarily of a series of heavy branches protruding from the trunk at right angles and then turning upwards.

The Black Cottonwood (*Populus trichocarpa*) is frequently found along stream beds or in damp places. It is a large deciduous tree with spreading branches tending to form a narrow, open, rounded crown. Trunks of mature trees are usually branchless for some distance. Leaves tend to turn yellow in the autumn. It must not be confused with the somewhat smaller Fremont Cottonwood (*Populus fremontii*) whose leaves are yellowish-green above and, although they have a flattened leaf stalk, do not flutter so obviously as do the leaves of the Aspen.

The Aspen (*Populus tremuloides*) is one of the most colorful high-mountain trees. It is a slender tree, irregularly branched, and usually found in close stands on slopes and mountain flats. Its green-white trunks with dull-green summer leaves that turn yellow in the autumn create a spectacular vista. Its flattened leaf stalks cause the leaves to flutter in the breeze, a readily recognizable characteristic of the Aspen.

The individual species of willows are rather difficult to identify by silhouette alone; however, the members of the Willow family are readily recognized by their shape and habitat. They are most frequently found along stream banks and in moist places from sea level to the high mountains. Some of the numerous species found in California are quite shrublike while others develop into sizable trees. Many species have a profusion of whiplike branches. Most species have long, narrow leaves.

The Red Willow (*Salix laevigata*), although occasionally somewhat shrubby, generally assumes treelike proportions. Its trunk is usually somewhat branched; however, it will commonly have one main trunk. Its branches form a somewhat irregular crown.

23

The Sandbar Willow (*Salix hindsiana*) is a small tree, frequently quite shrubby. It occurs usually along open ditches, on sand bars or flood beds.

The Valley Oak (*Quercus lobata*) is the largest of all California deciduous oaks. It is found throughout the central valleys and into the foothills. Its form varies greatly from tall, erect trees with rather sparse crowns and short outer drooping branches to those with wide-spreading branches and rather full crowns. The bark of the mature tree is usually thick, dark gray and checkered.

Interior Live Oak (*Quercus wislizenii*) is one of the common evergreen oaks of the Sierra Nevada foothills and lower mountain slopes. It is a beautiful tree, 25 to 75 feet tall, with spreading branches forming a rounded crown. To the casual observer it may be easily confused with the Coast Live Oak (*Quercus agrifolia*). However, on closer scrutiny, it will be noted that the branches of the Interior Live Oak are shorter and therefore, not as wide spreading as those of the Coast Live Oak. Hence, the crown of the Interior Live Oak is more compact and not as open as that of the Coast Live Oak.

The California Black Oak (*Quercus kelloggii*) is another spectacular deciduous oak which undoubtedly derived its name because of its very dark-colored bark. Leaves when first appearing on young shoots in the early spring may be bright pink to crimson. All leaves become shiny bright green as they mature and usually turn yellow to reddish in the fall, producing an interesting color effect on the California foothills and mountains. At lower elevations it is a graceful tree with a broad, rounded crown while at higher elevations it tends to be somewhat more irregularly branched and may, on occasion, develop an almost prostrate form.

The Big Leaf Maple (*Acer macrophyllum*) has a broad and rounded crown when found in the open, although usually not as compact as many introduced species. Under crowded conditions it may become quite rangy and ragged. Its dark green, deeply lobed leaves vary greatly in size. In deep shade some may be 12 or more inches wide, while in open sun some may be only about half that wide.

Blue Oak   Digger Pine   Interior Oak   Digger Pine   Canyon Oaks (cluster)   Valley Oak

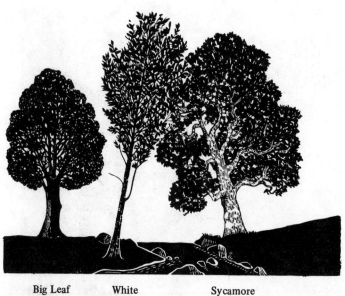

Big Leaf
Maple

White
Alder

Sycamore

The Box Elder (*Acer negundo*), when found in the open, is a medium-sized tree, usually with a short trunk and a broad, roundish crown, while in close stands it tends to become somewhat polelike and sparsely branched. Its leaves are pinnately compound in contrast to the simple leaves of the other native maples.

The White Alder (*Alnus rhombifolia*) is found along inland or mountain streams. It is readily recognized as a graceful tree with a clear and usually straight trunk, and open, spreading branches forming an oval crown. Its whitish- or grayish-brown bark is broken into irregular plates on old trees. Alders produce small woody cones. Careful observation is necessary to distinguish between the White and Red Alder (*Alnus oregona*).

The Western Sycamore (*Platanus racemosa*) is another of the more conspicuous native California trees and is usually found along old stream bottoms, banks of running streams, and canyons. Sycamores vary in form from tall, erect trees with heavy trunks to ones with large, crooked trunks and branches which nearly touch the ground. Bark on the lower trunks of old trees is thick, dark

| Madrone | California Buckeye | California Laurel (Bay) |

brown, and furrowed: on upper trunks and branches it is ashy-white and flaky, showing mottled colors of gray, brown, and yellowish- and dull-green. Leaves are pale green, large, and conspicuous.

The Madrone (*Arbutus menziesii*) is a handsome, much-branched broadleaf evergreen tree. It is easily recognized by its polished terra-cotta-colored bark which usually appears under dark brown and scaling older bark and by its dark, glossy green leaves, white flowers, and brilliant orange-red berrylike fruit.

The California Buckeye (*Aesculus californica*) is a small, compact tree which dots many of the dry slopes of our California mountains and foothills. The trees look like small green mounds on the hillsides shortly after the first winter rains; in the spring or early summer they are literally covered with clusters of white flowers, but by midsummer the leaves turn brown, producing yet a different hillside effect. By late summer or early fall the leaves have all dropped, leaving conspicuous pear-shaped pods hanging from the ends of its branches.

Box Elder   Western Redbud

The California Laurel (*Umbellularia californica*) is an interesting broadleaf evergreen tree which, when found in the open, produces a broad, rounded to modified pyramidal crown. When crowded it may develop a somewhat more open and irregular crown. In dry places, it may appear widely branched and somewhat shrubby. Its leaves have a distinctive green color which can readily be recognized at a distance.

The Western Redbud (*Cercis occidentalis*) is a small tree with a rounded crown that nearly reaches the ground. Its striking reddish-purple pealike flowers, which appear before the leaves, make it one of our most attractive flowering trees.

The Joshua Tree (*Yucca brevifolia*) is without doubt one of the most weird and unusual appearing desert trees. Young trees are without branches, while older trees are much branched, producing a widespread and open crown. Its long (7-to-12-inch), narrow, sharp, smooth, pale green leaves are clustered at the ends of the branches. Greenish-white flowers occur in dense compound clusters.

The Mojave Yucca (*Yucca schidigera*) is another strange desert tree, usually with a single unbranched trunk and with long, 1-to-3-foot, narrow, sharp leaves protruding in all directions. Its conspicuous creamy-white flowers are borne in a single, large, erect cluster.

Mojave Yucca   Joshua Tree

TREE DISTRIBUTION IN THE SIERRA NEVADA

For many years the life zone concept (first presented by C. Hart Merriam in 1898) has been used to account for plant and animal distribution in North America. In recent years botanists have turned to vegetation zones or plant communities and biologists and zoologists to biotic communities (based on plant communities but taking into account the occurrence of animal species as well) in efforts to account more adequately for the natural occurrence of plant and animal species. For details on this subject see *Introduction to California Plant Life* by Robert Ornduff, *Introduction to the Natural History of the San Francisco Bay Region* by Arthur C. Smith, *Introduction to the Natural History of Southern California* by Edmund C. Jaeger and Arthur C. Smith and *The Distribution of Forest Trees in California* by James R. Griffin and William B. Critchfield.

Much of the scientific and popular natural history writing of the period from the late 1890s through the early 1960s has included life zone designations for tree species. There is an extensive literature on life zones in the Sierra Nevada. Some schools still teach life zones as the basic explanation for plant and animal distribution. For these reasons life zone occurrence is given for each tree species in this book.

The life zones recognized by Merriam are as follows:

1. Lower Sonoran
2. Upper Sonoran
3. Transition
4. Canadian
5. Hudsonian
6. Boreal

In accordance with recent and current usage biotic communities have also been listed for each tree species. The authors have adopted the biotic communities for the Sierra Nevada as recognized by Arthur C. Smith (manuscript) and are indebted to him for the classification of biotic communities that appears below and for assistance in placing the Sierra Nevada tree species in the proper communities.

BIOTIC COMMUNITIES OF THE SIERRA NEVADA

1. Freshwater Marsh
2. Foothill Grassland
3. Riparian Woodland
4. Chaparral
5. Foothill Woodland
6. Yellow Pine (Ponderosa) Forest
7. Sierra Mixed Coniferous Forest
8. Sierran Lakes and Ponds
9. High Sierra Subalpine Forest
10. Bristlecone Pine Forest
11. Mountain Meadow
12. Alpine Fell
13. Sagebrush-Shadscale Scrub
14. Creosote Bush Scrub
15. Joshua Tree Woodland
16. Pinyon-Juniper Woodland
17. Sierra Rural
18. Sierra Urban

CONIFEROUS TREES

The conifers treated in this book are all narrow-leaf evergreen trees and include the pines, firs, false hemlocks, redwoods, cedars, cypresses, and junipers. Many species within these groups, such as the Douglas Fir, Western Yellow Pine, and Sugar Pine, are extremely important lumber trees. Less important, but of considerable commercial value, are the Jeffrey Pine, Lodgepole Pine, White Fir, and Incense Cedar. Other conifers are used for fuel, posts, pulp, and shoring. The lumber produced from conifers is relatively soft, strong, and light. It seasons well and works easily, making it by far the most important of all commercial woods. In view of its tremendous economic importance, large private lumber industries in the Pacific area are now actively engaged in an extensive reforestation program. The government is likewise concerned with controlled cutting in the National Forests, and in their reforestation. These practices will go far toward insuring a perpetual supply of this important commodity, as well as providing extensive recreational and limited grazing areas. In addition to their economic value, many conifers are extensively used as ornamental trees. Much of the forest area in the West is relatively marginal agricultural land. However, it will produce forest trees and it is therefore important that the best forest practices be established and maintained.

Since the flowers of conifers are not distinctive, they are not described in the following accounts, although months of flowering are given. The fruit of all conifers described in this volume, except that of the junipers, are woody cones. The junipers produce a berrylike fruit, which, although not woody, is morphologically a cone. The size and characteristics of all cones described are those of the ripe cone.

PINE FAMILY (PINACEAE)

The Pine family includes more members than any other family of native cone-bearing trees in California. The members (genera) of this large family included in this book are pines (*Pinus*), false hemlock (*Pseudotsuga*), hemlock (*Tsuga*) and firs (*Abies*).

Pines (*Pinus*)

There are thirteen different species of native pines growing in the Sierra Nevada: some are rare and geographically quite restricted, others are common and widespread. Some, such as the Western Yellow Pine and the Sugar Pine, are important lumber trees, while others have little commercial value. Pines are distinguished from other members of the family by the fact that their needlelike leaves occur in bundles of one to five enclosed at the base by a sheath of papery scales. Cones ripen during the second or third season.

For the purpose of identification we will divide the pines into groups based on the number of leaves in a bundle, and henceforth, will refer to these leaves as needles.

One-Needle Pines

One-Leaf Pinyon Pine *(Pinus monophylla)*

This pine is commonly known as one of the nut pines since its seeds are large and edible. The nuts were extensively gathered by Indians who lived in the area and used them as an important item of food. The cones, when mature, open and disperse their seeds over some little distance, which made gathering the crop a rather tedious task. Moreover, when the seeds were thus scattered, keen-eyed birds, squirrels, and other animals were quick to discover their presence. However, the Indians eventually learned that if the cones were gathered just before they were ripe, dried, and then placed around a fire, they would open and release their seeds. They also discovered that the heat made the seeds more

One-Leaf Pinyon Pine

palatable and that it was a great deal easier to gather the seeds from around the fire than from the grass in competition with the birds and squirrels.

The Pinyon Pine is an extremely slow-growing, small, and symmetrical tree, usually not more than 30 feet tall; many trees reach an age of over two hundred years. In recent years Pinyon Pines have been extensively harvested as Christmas trees. Residential subdivisions are also making inroads into its natural habitats. Unless these practices are controlled, we will soon find this beautiful little tree reaching a point of extinction. To forestall such a catastrophe, efforts should be initiated to have certain remaining undisturbed areas set aside as public reservations.

Leaves and fruit: Needles usually in ones, not in bundles, 1 to 2 inches long, stiff, and slightly curved towards the stem. The cones mature in August of the second growing season. Seeds are dark chocolate-brown and about 1/2 inch long.

Range: Eastern dry slope and ridges of the Sierra Nevada at elevations of 3,500 to 9,000 feet, from Alpine County south; also, in a few scattered locations on the western slope of the Sierra Nevada from Tuolumne County south, frequently found with the California Juniper. May. Pinyon-Juniper Woodland. Upper Sonoran Zone.

Two-Needle Pines

Lodgepole Pine (*Pinus contorta* var. *murrayana*)

Also known as Tamarack Pine, this is a tall and slender tree when found in dense stands, heavier and branched in open stands, 50 to 100 ft. tall. Its bark is thin and covered with small scales. The wood is light, soft, and straight-grained and is used extensively for poles, railroad ties, mine timbers, box shooks, laths, and pulp. Fire and pine beetle cause heavy losses annually. It is rarely seen in cultivation. Cones, either natural or sprayed with silver or gold paint, make attractive Christmas decorations.

Leaves and fruit: Yellow-green needles in twos, 1 to 2 1/2 in. long, and stiff. Cones 1 to 2 in. long, abundant; cone scales tipped with short, slender prickles.

Range: Widespread in borders of high mountain meadows and slopes from the San Jacinto Mountains north through the Sierra Nevada to Alaska at elevations of 5,000 to 11,000 ft. July. Sierra Mixed Coniferous Forest. Canadian Zone.

Three-Needle Pines

Western Yellow Pine (*Pinus ponderosa*) Plate 1, *b.*

The Western Yellow Pine, also known as Ponderosa Pine, is one of our most important lumber trees. Mature specimens vary greatly in size and appearance due to variations in soil and climatic conditions. Under ideal conditions some trees may attain a height of 200 ft. and a diameter of 5 to 6 ft. Under less favorable conditions, a height of only 70 to 80 ft. and a diameter of 16 to 20 in. may be its limit. Bark characteristics also vary greatly from large tawny-yellow or russet-brown platelets to hard, dark, and deeply furrowed ridges on young trees or trees growing under less favorable conditions. Specimens showing the latter bark characteristics are frequently known as "bull pine."

Leaves and fruit: Yellow-green needles in threes, 5 to 10 in. long and densely clustered at the ends of branches. Cones 2 to 5 in. long, quite symmetrical, open, light-weight; scales of mature cones tipped with outturned pin-point prickles, which prick one's

35

hands when they are cupped around the cone.

Range: Widespread in the Sierra Nevada at elevations of 2,000 to 8,500 ft. Frequently it is the predominant tree in the area where it occurs. May-June. Yellow Pine Forest. Transition Zone.

Jeffrey Pine (*Pinus jeffreyi*) Plate 1, *c.*

This pine, 60 to 180 ft. tall, is quite similar in many respects to Western Yellow Pine, and is considered by some authors to be a variety of this species. It is also known to hybridize with the Western Yellow Pine. There are however, sufficient differences — cones, silhouette, bark, and habitat — to justify two distinct species. The bark of mature trees is usually dark reddish-brown and broken into irregular scaly plates. The deep furrows in the bark, when warmed in the sun, emit a pineapple- or vanilla-scented odor. Western Yellow Pine emits no such odor. Crowns tend to be longer and more symmetrical than those of the Yellow Pine. Lumber is quite similar to that of Yellow Pine.

Leaves and fruit: Blue-green needles in threes, 5 to 10 in. long. Foliage tends to be heavier and more dense than that of the Yellow Pine. Cones 5 to 10 in. long, proportionately heavier and bulkier than those of the Yellow Pine; prickles on ends of mature cone scales are slightly incurved and usually do not prick hands when they are cupped around ripe cones.

Washoe Pine (*Pinus washoensis*)

This relatively rare tree is similar to the Jeffrey Pine but with significant differences, the most apparent of which are the smaller cones and shorter needles. A height of 180 ft. and diameter of 3 ft. can be attained while in other stands it grows only to 90 ft. In the Warner Mountains, Modoc County, north of the Sierra Nevada, the tree reaches diameters of 4 ft. On mature specimens the bark is roughly fissured; however, a few can be found showing the plated structure.

Leaves and fruits: Gray-green needles in threes, 4 to 6 in. long. Cones 2 to slightly over 3 in. long, with prickles on the end, like the Jeffrey Pine, slightly incurved.

Range: A small area on the east slope of Mount Rose, north-west of Lake Tahoe and a second stand near Babbitt Peak, which is a part of the Bald Mountain Range some 20 miles northwest of Mount Rose at elevations from 7,000 to almost 9,000 ft. May-June. Sierra Mixed Coniferous Forest. Transition and Canadian Zones.

Digger Pine (*Pinus sabiniana*) Plate 1, *d*.

The Digger Pine, 50 to 70 ft. tall, is the first native conifer that one sees when entering the hot dry foothills of the Sierra Nevada from the Central Valley. It is readily identified by its characteristic gray-green needles, large cones, and forked trunk. It owes its common name to the fact that its large seeds were an important item of food for the California Digger Indians. The wood is coarse-grained and has no real lumber value, but it is used for fuel.

Leaves and fruit: Gray-green needles in threes, 7 to 13 in. long and usually drooping from the ends of the branches. Light brown cones 6 to 10 in. long and sometimes almost as broad. Cone scales end in a sharp, often hooklike spur. Cones may remain on the tree for several seasons after the seeds have been shed.

Range: Dry foothills and lower mountain slopes bordering the Central Valley at elevations below 4,500 ft. Frequently associated with the Blue Oak. April-May. Foothill Woodland. Upper Sonoran Zone.

Knobcone Pine (*Pinus attenuata*) Plate 2, *a*.

A small, slender tree, 20 to 50 ft. tall, which usually has an open, rounded top. It is one of our most unusual trees from the standpoint of survival. Its cones, which adhere to the trunk or branches indefinitely, rarely open except in case of fire. Here, then, is a tree which depends almost entirely on a major catastrophe for its propagation. It is a spectacular sight to visit a Knobcone Pine forest which has recently been ravished by a fire and see the hundreds of cones on each tree popped wide open. If the fire was fast moving and not too hot, many of the seeds that had been released would germinate and produce trees that would then be affected by the next fire. The wood is light, soft, and coarse-grained.

37

Leaves and fruit: Pale yellow-green, slender needles in threes, 3 to 5 in. long. Unsymmetrical cones 4 to 6 in. long and in whorls. Cone scales on the outer side and near the base have a pyramidal apex which is armed with a prickle.

Range: Dry and barren western slope of the Sierra Nevada below 4,000 ft. as far south as Tulare County. March-May. Foothill Woodland, Yellow Pine Forest. Upper Sonoran and Transition Zones.

Five-Needle Pines

Sugar Pine (*Pinus lambertiana*) Plate 2, *b.*

The Sugar Pine is the largest of all pines. A mature tree may reach a height of over 200 ft. and a diameter of 6 to 7 ft. In the southern part of its range it is somewhat smaller. It is one of our most magnificent cone-bearing trees, and also the one which is the most easily recognized. The trunks of the mature trees are straight and only slightly tapering until its long, horizontal branches, which tend to form a flat crown, are reached. Young trees are gracefully symmetrical. Its large cones, either single, in twos, or occasionally in threes, hang pendant from the ends of the branches and serve to identify the tree from long distances. These cones are the longest of all pines and they ripen during the late summer of the second season, shed their seeds in the late fall, and usually drop during the late winter, spring, or early summer of the third season. The bark of mature trees is reddish-brown to purplish-gray, deeply furrowed, and with the ridges broken into irregular scaly plates; bark of young trees is dark gray and smooth. Wood is light, soft, straight-grained, and relatively free of knots. It is extensively used where a wood of superior quality is required and consequently it commands a high price. Prudent harvesting and utilization must be exercised in order to extend as long as possible the availability of this very desirable wood. Unfortunately, it is disappearing faster than it is being replenished by even our most modern conservation techniques.

Leaves and fruit: Blue-green needles in fives, 3 to 4 in. long, usually sharp-pointed and clustered tassel-like at end of branches.

Cones 12 to 20 in. long and 4 to 5 in. in diameter.

Range: Abundant on western slope of the Sierra Nevada at elevations of 2,500 to 9,000 feet. May-June. Yellow Pine Forest. Sierra Mixed Coniferous Forest. Transition Zone.

Western White Pine (*Pinus monticola*)

Also known as Silver Pine and occasionally as Little Sugar Pine. The latter name undoubtedly evolved because of certain similiarities between the two species. A forest tree up to 150 ft. tall with a slender short-branched symmetrical crown when young or in close stands tending to become open and spreading with age, especially when in open stands. Cones are borne in clusters of one to six on the ends of top branches. Mature cones are somewhat similar to those of the Sugar Pine except smaller, lighter and curved. Bark on trunk of mature trees brownish and usually broken into small squarish, flaky plates. Bark on young tree, silvery gray and smooth.

Leaves and fruit: Blue-green needles in fives, 2 to 4 in. long, and usually bluntish. Cones 6 to 8 in. long and 2 1/2 to 3 1/2 in. in diameter.

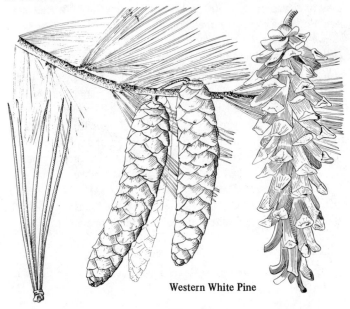

Western White Pine

Range: Scattered in Sierra Nevada at elevations of 6,000 to 10,000 ft. June-July. Sierra Mixed Coniferous Forest, High Sierra Subalpine Forest. Canadian Zone.

Bristlecone Pine (*Pinus aristata*)[1] Plate 2, *c.*

Also known as Hickory Pine, this is a medium-sized tree, 20 to 50 ft. tall, sometimes with a short, thick trunk. Its deep green foliage which is clustered near the ends of the branches tends to give the tree a bushy appearance. Bark on old trunks is dull reddish-brown, on young trunks and branches smooth and whitish. It is another of our interesting high mountain pines. Until 1956 the Sequoias were considered to be our oldest living trees, but then 4,000-year-old Bristlecone Pines were found in the White Mountains with cores of some specimens showing an age of 4,600 years.

Leaves and fruit: Dark green needles in fives, 1 to 1 1/2 in. long, lustrous on upper and whitish on under surface. Ovoid cones purplish-brown, nearly sessile, 2 1/2 to 3 1/2 in. long. Cone scales thickened at apex and armed with a fragile straight prickle.

Range: Dry rocky slopes of Inyo, Panamint, and White mountains at elevations of 7,500 to 11,500 ft. June-July. Bristlecone Pine Forest. Canadian Zone.

Limber Pine (*Pinus flexilis*)

This is a low, thick-trunked, and much-branched tree, 25 to 50 ft. tall. Its crown consists of long drooping branches, which, in the case of young trees, sometimes nearly reaches the ground. Branchlets are pliable and tough, which undoubtedly accounts for its name. Bark on mature trees is blackish or dark brown, on young trees whitish-gray. It is one of the less well-known pines, due doubtless to its high, relatively inaccessible range.

Leaves and fruit: Dark green needles in fives, 1 1/2 to 3 in. long stiff, and clustered tassel-like at the ends of the branches, cones 3 to 8 in. long. Tips of cone scales greatly thickened and often curved.

---

[1] The name *Pinus longaeva* has been proposed for the western race of this species.

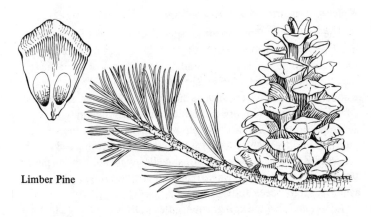

Limber Pine

Range: Eastern slope of Sierra Nevada south of Mono Pass at elevations of 7,500 to 11,600 ft., in the Panamint, Inyo and White ranges. July-August. High Sierra Subalpine Forest, Bristlecone Pine Forest. Canadian and Boreal Zones.

Foxtail Pine (*Pinus balfouriana*) Plate 2, *d.*

The Foxtail Pine is another interesting but somewhat restricted high mountain pine, 20 to 45 ft. tall. It has a bushy crown of irregular long branches, lower branches are usually shorter and stout. Bark on mature trees is irregularly fissured and somewhat flaky, varies in color from a cinnamon-brown to a grayish-tan. Bark on new growth is smooth and whitish. Bright blue-green appressed and dense foliage covers ends of branches for a distance of 10 or more inches effecting a foxtail-like appearance, hence, its common name.

Leaves and fruit: Needles in fives, 3/4 to 1 1/2 in. long, dark blue-green on upper surface, whitish on under surface, stiff and curved, dense and appressed at ends of branches. Cones 2 to 5 in. long, slender before opening, purple to reddish-brown, scales thickened at apex and armed with a pinpoint prickle.

Range: Dry slopes and ridges of Tulare and Inyo counties of Sierra Nevada at 6,000 to 11,500 ft. July. High Sierra Subalpine. Forest. Hudsonian Zone.

Whitebark Pine (*Pinus albicaulis*) Plate 3, *a*.

The Whitebark Pine is another spectacular windswept timber-line tree. Down through the years they have been pounded by the fierce alpine winds and pressed down by heavy snowpacks so that they may rise only a few feet above the ground, but their trunks may stretch out along the surface for a number of feet. Under protected and more favorable conditions they may develop into trees 20 to 50 ft. tall, with spreading flexible branches and frequently with twisted or crooked trunks. Bark on branches is reddish-brown to reddish-yellow. Its reddish-purple staminate catkins produce a striking effect when silhouetted against its dark green foliage.

Leaves and fruit: Dark green needles in fives, 1 to 2 1/2 in. long, dense, and stiff. Cones ovoid to subglobose, 1 to 3 in. long, dark purple, very resinous; scales thickened at apex and often terminated with a blunt point.

Range: Dry, rocky areas at 8,000 to 12,000 ft. in Sierra Nevada from Tulare County north. Also, Modoc and Siskiyou counties to British Columbia and Alberta. July and August. High Sierra Subalpine Forest. Hudsonian Zone.

False Hemlock (*Pseudotsuga*)

There is only one native false hemlock in the Sierra Nevada — the Douglas Fir. Young trees, when growing in open stands, tend to form graceful pyramidal silhouettes with long, drooping branches. Their flat, soft, and abundant needlelike leaves tend to give the trees a full and lacy appearance. The needles spiral completely around the twig, but usually appear two-ranked, due to very short twisted green petioles. Cones mature in one season.

Douglas Fir (*Pseudotsuga menziesii*) Plate 3, *b*.

This is a large forest tree, 150 to 300 ft. tall, often with a massive clear trunk up to 100 feet or more. Douglas Firs in the southern part of their range are somewhat smaller. The typical pyramidal crown of a young tree with its horizontal and sometimes drooping branches tends to become rounded or somewhat flattened with maturity or in thick stands. Bark of mature trees is dark, furrowed, thick, and corky. Bark of young trees is smooth and grayish. It is our most important lumber tree and is commonly known in the trade as Oregon Pine, an erroneous name reputedly attributed to early midwestern lumbermen who came from an area where fir was a decidedly inferior lumber tree. Small trees are used extensively as Christmas trees and widely planted as ornamentals.

Leaves and fruit: Leaves 3/4 to 1 1/2 in. long and about 1/16th in. wide, flat, blunt, blue-green on top, with two grayish bands beneath and very short twisted petioles; leaves persist for 8 to 10 years. Cones 2 to 4 in. long, numerous, pendulous, and with conspicuous three-pointed bracts protruding between the cone scales.

Range: Widely distributed in the Sierra Nevada from Fresno County north at elevations of 2,500 to 6,000 ft. Yellow Pine Forest. Upper Sonoran and Transition Zones.

Hemlock (*Tsuga*)

There are only two species of native hemlocks found in California — Western or Coast Hemlock, a native of northwestern California, and the Mountain Hemlock, which occurs in the Sierra Nevada.

Mountain Hemlock (*Tsuga mertensiana*) Plate 3, c.

Mountain Hemlock is a beautiful high mountain tree, 60 to 125 ft. tall, with graceful and open pyramidal crown terminating in a long drooping leader, even in quite large and mature trees. Branches loaded with bluish-green foliage will cover the tree almost to its base giving it a characteristic lacy appearance. With age the crown tends to spread and become somewhat irregular. Leaves are attached to tiny woody pegs, which persist after the leaves disappear giving the twig a rough appearance. This is a point of difference between the hemlock and false hemlocks and firs, whose leaves are not attached to pegs. The hard and deeply furrowed scaly bark on mature trees is a dark gray to a deep

43

reddish brown. On young branches the bark is a light reddish brown and densely pubescent for 2 to 3 years.

Leaves and fruit: Leaves glossy bluish green, typically less than 1 in. long, extending from all sides of the branchlets, but they appear somewhat two-ranked due to a twist at the base of the leaf; upper surface convex or grooved, lower surface rounded. Cones 1-3 in. long, sessile, narrowed towards apex and base, bracts not extending beyond cone scales.

Range: Sierra Nevada from Fresno County north at 6,000 to 11,000 ft. Sierra Mixed Coniferous Forest, High Sierra Subalpine Forest. Hudsonian Zone.

Firs (*Abies*)

There are only two native firs in the Sierra Nevada — the White Fir and the Red Fir. Firs are tall evergreen trees with characteristic conical crowns. Young trees when not crowded are beautifully symmetrical. Branches grow in whorls at regular intervals around the trunk. The erect cones are borne near the ends of the upper branches; they mature in one season and disintegrate on the trees. Firs are extensively sold as Christmas trees. Christmas tree farms are becoming common in California and should be encouraged as they reduce the indiscriminate cutting of young native trees. Firs produce lumber of varying quality and are considered important forest trees.

White Fir (*Abies concolor*) Plate 3, *d.*

White Firs are tall, large forest trees 60 to 200 ft. tall. The crowns of mature trees tend to be roundish while those of young trees are pyramidal. Bark on the trunk of mature trees is deeply furrowed and ash-gray. Bark on upper branches and on young trees is smooth and grayish. They are frequently sold on the Christmas tree market under the erroneous name of "Silvertip." The wood is light, soft, and rather coarse-grained. It is used extensively as dimension lumber and as box wood. The wood tends to punk when exposed to excessive moisture. The twist at the base of the leaf serves with other characteristics to distinguish it from the Red Fir or true "Silvertip" whose leaves have no twist at their base. It is extensively planted as an ornamental.

Leaves and fruit: Leaves 1 to 2 in. long; leaves on lower branches longer than those on upper branches, about 1/8 in. wide; may be pointed, rounded, or slightly notched at apex, bluish green; two whitish brands on under surface separated by greenish keel; twisted base causing leaves to appear two-ranked. Cones 2 to 5 in. high, erect on ends of upper branches.

Range: Main timber belt of the Sierra Nevada at elevations of 3,000 to 8,300 ft. June. Yellow Pine Forest, Sierra Mixed Coniferous Forest. Transition Zone.

Red Fir (*Abies magnifica*) Plate 4, *a.*

The Red Fir is a high mountain forest tree, 60 to 180 ft. tall. Young trees are readily recognized by their symmetrical shape, narrow pyramidal crowns composed of numerous horizontal tiers of short branches and deep blue-green foliage. It is one of the most beautiful young trees in the forest. Crowns of older trees tend to become roundish and sometimes even somewhat irregular. Bark on young trees is whitish and quite smooth, on mature trees it is dark reddish brown and roughly fissured. It is the true Silvertip and can readily be distinguished from the White Fir by the fact that its somewhat four-sided leaves are not twisted at the base, while those of the White Fir are twisted.

Leaves and fruit: Leaves 3/4 to 1 1/2 inches long, curved upward on upper branches usually somewhat two-ranked on lower branches; stomates on each surface; tips rounded and not notched; new leaves glaucous green later becoming deep blue-green. Cones 5 to 8 in. long, erect on ends of branches.

Range: Sierra Nevada at 5,000 to 9,000 ft. June. Sierra Mixed Coniferous Forest. Canadian Zone.

Redwood Family (*Taxodiaceae*)

Two native species of redwoods are found in California today. Fossil evidence indicates that these species as well as several others now extinct were once widespread in North America,

45

, and Asia. Once considered to be the oldest living things
h, redwoods are now placed second, behind the Bristlecone
Pine. Redwoods are still considered the earth's largest living
things. The Coast Redwood is found only in the coastal fog belt
from Santa Lucia Mountains to southwest Oregon. Sierra
Redwood or Giant Sequoia is confined to the central Sierra
Nevada. Both species may be found as garden or street trees in
many California cities.

Giant Sequoia, Big Tree or Sierra Redwood (*Sequoiadendron giganteum*)
Plate 4, *b*.

The mature Giant Sequoia is easily the monarch of the Sierra
Nevada forests and one of the most magnificent trees in the world.
It is readily recognized by its orange-tan to cinnamon-red thick
fibrous bark and its massive branchless trunks. Young trees have
a beautiful pyramidal crown which tends to become rounded and
broken with age, resulting ultimately in a crown consisting of a
relatively few heavy spreading horizontal and upturned branches.

The bark is thick, 10 to 24 in., on mature trees. It is fibrous,
nonresinous, nearly noninflammable, and forms an almost asbes-
toslike protection against fire. However, successive fires have in
many instances burned through to the heartwood, but because
the heartwood is also nonresinous and does not burn readily the
effect is not always fatal. Numerous spectacular examples showing the results of fire are evident in Sequoia National Park. The
Telescope Tree has a large part of its heartwood burned out leaving a chimney through which blue sky can be seen. The Room
Tree is one in which fires have burned out the interior leaving
openings on two sides. These fire-scarred giants, showing extensive burn on the thin shells that support the trees, are only two of
many illustrations of the effectiveness of the Sierra Redwood in
resisting fire.

Giant Sequoias do not stump sprout as do the Coast Redwoods, hence, they must depend on seeds for reproduction.
They, like the Coast Redwoods, have no taproot but numerous
large lateral roots and a mass of feeder roots that lie near the surface. To protect these roots, which are the lifeline of the tree, it
is important that the area around the tree be kept free from arti-

ficial encroachments such as camping, tramping, and the construction of paved trails and roadways. In many parks, barricades have been erected around the bases of certain trees in order to preserve as nearly as possible a natural habitat and to protect them from the onslaught of careless visitors. This practice is to be respected and encouraged.

The wood is light, quite brittle, and very durable. Giant Sequoias are frequently planted as ornamentals.

Leaves and fruit: Leaves are awl-shaped, 1/8 to 1/2 in. long partly overlapping each other, thickly covering the stem, pointed tips spreading out more or less from the twig. Cones 2 to 3 in. long with thick woody scales.

Range: Western slope of the Sierra Nevada in scattered groves from Placer County to Tulare County at 4,000 to 8,000 ft. Yellow Pine Forest, Sierra Mixed Coniferous Forest. Transition Zone.

Cypress Family (*Cupressaceae*)

The members (genera) of the Cypress family found in the Sierra Nevada are Incense Cedar (*Calocedrus,* cypresses (*Cupressus*), and junipers (*Juniperus*). They include many valuable and picturesque species which are widespread throughout the state. Many species are extensively cultivated in parks and gardens. They all have closely adhering scalelike leaves.

Incense Cedar (*Calocedrus decurrens*)[2] Plate 4, *c.*

The Incense Cedar is a handsome, aromatic evergreen, 75 to 150 ft. tall, with a tapering trunk covered with thick fibrous cinnamon-brown bark, which somewhat resembles the trunk and bark of the Giant Sequoia. Young trees are pyramidal. The crowns of the older trees are open and irregular. Leaf-bearing twigs tend to branch in one plane forming flat sprays which give the tree a lacy appearance. The wood is light, soft, and durable. It is used extensively in making shingles, posts, lead pencils, railroad ties, and many other useful products.

---

[2] Formerly *Libocedrus.*

Leaves and fruit: Leaves simple, scale-shaped, 1/8 to 3/16 in. long, closely appressed to the branchlets, only the tips free; cyclic, four-ranked, two outer rows keel-shaped and overlapping the two inner rows; highly aromatic when crushed. Cones ¾ to 1 in. long consisting of one pair of large seed-bearing scales separated from a closed center of 2 or 4 sharp-pointed scales, pendulous, maturing the first season.

Range: Main timber belt of Sierra Nevada at 1,800 to 7,000 ft. April-May. Yellow Pine Forest, Sierra Mixed Coniferous Forest. Transition Zone.

Cypress (*Cupressus*)

There are ten cypresses native to California, two of which are found in the Sierra Nevada. All produce woody, generally globular cones, which mature the second season and may remain on the tree for several seasons.

MacNab Cypress (*Cupressus macnabiana*) Plate 4, *d*.

The MacNab cypress is a small tree, 15 to 40 ft. tall, sometimes bushy and sometimes with open pyramidal crown. Bark on young trees rich brown, later grayish with flat connecting ridges. Foliage gray-green with pungent and somewhat aromatic odor.

Leaves and fruit: Leaves scalelike, obtuse with conspicuous dorsal pits, opposite and thickly covering the branches. Cones ¾ to 1 in. long, reddish brown, upper pair of scales usually armed with conical or hooked umbos.

Range: Dry foothills of Sierra Nevada from Amador County to Butte County at 1,000 to 2,600 ft. Foothill Woodland, Chaparral. Upper Sonoran, Transition Zones.

Piute Cypress (*Cupressus nevadensis*)

Piute Cypress is a small erect tree, 20 to 30 ft. tall, with a broad pyramidal crown. Old bark gray brown and fibrous. Young bark reddish to brownish. Foliage soft gray-green and glaucous.

Leaves and fruit: Leaves scalelike, acute with active dorsal glands. Cones light gray-brown, 3/4 to 1 1/4 in. long, 6 to 8 scales with somewhat conical umbos.

Range: Dry slopes at 4,000 to 6,000 ft. on Piute Mountains. Foothill Woodland. Upper Sonoran Zone.

Juniper (*Juniperus*)

Junipers are closely related to the cypresses, and it is often difficult to distinguish between the two genera without studying their fruits. The fruit of the juniper is an ovoid berrylike cone, usually covered with coalesced scales, while the fruit of the cypress is a globular or subglobular woody cone. Both mature the second season.

Western Juniper (*Juniperus occidentalis*)

Also known as Sierra Juniper. This is a very picturesque tree, 20 to 60 ft. tall, often with a gnarled and grotesque form. It is one of the real monarchs of the high mountains and is readily recognized by its short, stocky, weatherbeaten, shreddy cinnamon-brown trunk and open crown. Young trees in protected areas have a straight, sharply tapering open crown.

Leaves and fruit: Gray-green scalelike leaves, about 1/8 in. long, attached singly in circles of three, closely appressed, completely covering the twig and forming a rounded stem with six longitudinal rows of leaves; each leaf marked on the back with a glandular resin pit. Cones berrylike, 1/4 to 1/3 in. long, globular to oblong-ovoid, bluish black with white bloom at maturity.

Range: Sierra Nevada on windswept ridges and granite creices at 6,500 to 11,000 ft. Sierra Mixed Coniferous Forest, High Sierra Subalpine Forest, Pinyon-Juniper Woodland. Canadian Zone.

California Juniper (*Juniperus californica*)

A small tree, 20 to 30 ft. tall, usually with several secondary trunks emerging from near the base and with a broad open crown.

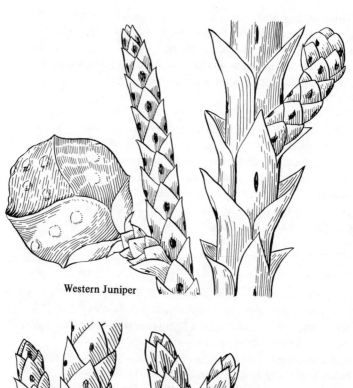

Western Juniper

California Juniper

Bark is ashy-gray in contrast to the cinnamon-brown bark of the Western Juniper, with which it is sometimes confused.

Leaves and fruit: Scalelike leaves similar to those of the Western Juniper except more bluntish. Cones berrylike, globose to oblong, 3/8 to 5/8 in. long, reddish brown under whitish bloom when mature.

Range: Western slope of Sierra Nevada in Tulare and Kern counties. January-March. Foothill Woodland, Joshua Tree Woodland, Pinyon-Juniper Woodland. Upper Sonoran Zone.

Utah Juniper (*Juniperus osteosperma*) Plate 5, *a*.

This is a small tree or treelike shrub, 10 to 15 ft. tall, usually with a short or several-stemmed trunk, sometimes called Desert Juniper. It is very similar to California Juniper except that it ordinarily has a rounded crown, giving the appearance of small round green clumps on the hillsides.

Leaves and fruit: Scale-shaped leaves, 1/10 to 1/8 in. long, tending to be sharp-pointed, attached singly in circles of 2 or 3 around the twig, usually without glands. Cones berrylike, globular, 3/16 to 3/8 in. long, reddish brown under whitish bloom when mature.

Range: Associated with One-Leaf Pinyon Pine on dry slopes and flats at 4,800 to 8,500 feet from east Mojave Desert to Bridgeport area. Pinyon-Juniper Woodland, Joshua Tree Woodland. Upper Sonoran Zone.

Yew Family (*Taxaceae*)

Two members (genera) of the Yew Family, namely Yew (*Taxus*) and California Nutmeg (*Torreya*) are found in the Sierra Nevada. They are evergreen trees or shrubs with simple narrow leaves spirally arranged, but which usually appear two-ranked due to a twist at the base of the leaf. Plants dioecious, fruit drupe-like, composed of a hard seed surrounded by a fleshy envelope.

Western Yew (*Taxus brevifolia*) Plate 5, *b*.

The Western Yew is a small evergreen tree, 15 to 40 ft. tall, or occasionally taller. Horizontal drooping branches form flat sprays. Bark reddish brown and sometimes shreddy. Wood strong, hard and durable, wears smooth as ebony with use. Used by early Indians for making bows, paddles, and spear handles. Heartwood beautiful rose-red, sapwood clear yellow. Scarce, hence of little real commercial importance.

Leaves and fruit: Leaves simple, 1/2 to 3/4 in. long, 1/16 in. wide; thinnish, acute, short-pointed; deep yellow-green above, paler beneath. Fruit berrylike, red, fleshy, cup-shaped, nearly enclosing a lone seed.

Range: West slope of Sierra Nevada from Tulare County north below 7,000 ft. April-May. Yellow Pine Forest, Sierra Mixed Coniferous Forest. Canadian and Transition Zones.

California Nutmeg (*Torreya californica*) Plate 5, *c*.

The California Nutmeg is an evergreen tree, 15 to 90 ft. tall, with slender spreading whorled branches, with stiff, dark green, simple, linear and sharp-pointed leaves. It resembles the Yew in general appearance but its leaves are larger, stiffer and distinctly more sharp-pointed. It is sometimes known as Stinking Cedar because of the fetid odor given off when leaves or bark are bruised. Bark, thin, ashy to yellowish brown, loosely scaly, underbark is gray-brown tinted with orange. Wood, soft, close-grained and light. Heartwood yellow, sapwood thin and nearly white. Sometimes planted as a park tree for its dark green foliage and green plumlike seeds.

Leaves and fruit: Leaves simple, 1 to 2 1/2 in. long, 1/16 to 1/8 in. wide; flat, stiff, spiny-pointed; deep dark green above, paler beneath with two narrow glaucous bands of stamata. Fruit drupelike, green with purplish markings, 1 to 1 3/4 in. long. Single seed with woody outer coat completely surrounded with a thin fleshy covering.

Range: Western slope of Sierra Nevada from Tulare to Tehama counties below 4,500 ft. April-May. Yellow Pine Forest. Transition Zone.

BROADLEAF TREES

The Sierra Nevada has a variety of native broadleaf trees. The most common are the alders, maples, oaks, poplars, sycamore, and willows. There are also many unusual or spectacular species such as the dogwoods, elderberries, Madrone, California Laurel and yuccas, to mention just a few. At certain times of the year the buckeyes, dogwoods, elderberries, flannel bushes, oaks, poplars, redbuds, toyons and yuccas add much to the color of the California landscape by the varied and brilliant hues of their flowers, fruits, or foliage. Most native broadleaf trees in California except certain oaks and maples, have comparatively little commercial value except for firewood and novelties. However, many have real esthetic value and are cultivated extensively as street or park trees. Undoubtedly their greatest value lies in the beauty and charm which they lend to the California landscape. What is more picturesque than the rolling foothills dotted with spreading Interior Live Oak, Blue Oak, and Digger Pine or the moist high mountain slopes covered in the fall of the year with a blanket of bright yellow Quaking Aspen silhouetted against a background of green pine or fir, or the brilliant red coloration of the Mountain Dogwood after the first onset of cold weather? Every legitimate effort should be made to preserve as much as possible of California's natural beauty consistent with a well-developed overall utilization pattern, recognizing that nature once destroyed can never be reestablished within one's lifetime.

Leaf descriptions as used in this section refer to the characteristics of the leaf blade only unless otherwise indicated.

AGAVE FAMILY (AGAVACEAE)

Joshua Tree (*Yucca brevifolia*) Plate 6, *a.*

An unusual looking tree, 15 to 30 ft tall. Mature trees have a columnar trunk with many thick and bristly branches. Young trees are without branches until they produce their first flowers, then frequently two branches develop, each of which will generally produce two more branches, continuing thus until a much-branched and open crown is formed. The bark, where free of leaves, is reddish brown to gray and checked into small squarish plates. The sharp-pointed bayonetlike leaves, which adhere to the stem and branches for many years, discourage intrusion from would-be large animals who, in this otherwise barren area, would feed on its foliage. This protective provision is one factor which has made possible the survival of this fascinating tree.

It is easily the most weird denizen of the California deserts. The approach to a Joshua Tree forest on a bright moonlit night presents a never-to-be-forgotten sight. The federal government has set aside the Joshua Tree National Monument to preserve the trees in their natural habitat.

Leaves, flowers, and fruit: Leaves bluish green, stiff, 6 to 10 in. long, 2 in. or less wide at the base, tapering to very sharp points, edges with minute teeth throughout, persisting for many years. Stems and branches, except old trunks, covered with close thatch of dead leaves. Flowers greenish white, fleshy, waxen, rather ill-smelling, about 2 in. long, borne at the end of the crown branches in a single stiff and branched cluster about 1 ft. long. Fruit is a capsule, 2 to 4 in. long, plumb, with 6 chambers filled with flat black seeds, becoming dry and dropping when mature, scattered by wind.

Range: Mojave Desert regions of Inyo County and eastern Kern County at 2,000 to 6,000 ft. elevation. April-May. Joshua Tree Woodland. Lower Sonoran Zone.

Mojave Yucca (*Yucca schidigera*) Plate 6, *b*.

Also known as Spanish Dagger. A small strange tree, 5 to .15 ft. tall, with a single or occasionally branched trunk. The bark, where free of dead leaves, is dark brown, cross-checked, and furrowed. This is another unusual tree, indigenous to the hot arid areas of southern California.

Leaves, flowers, and fruit: Leaves yellow-green, 1 1/2 to 3 ft. long, 2 to 3 in. wide at base, tapering to sharp point, margins entire with few curled shreddy filaments, stiff. Flowers, white to cream, borne in a single-branched cluster, 1 to 1 1/2 ft. long. Fruit is a capsule, 2 to 4 in. long, with 6 chambers filled with black seeds.

Range: Dry rocky slopes and mesas usually below 7,000 ft. on western edge of Mojave Desert. April-May. Sagebrush-Shadscale Scrub, Creosote Bush Scrub. Lower Sonoran Zone.

WILLOW FAMILY (SALICACEAE)

The willow family includes two genera, the poplars and the willows. Members of this family produce spikelike masses of flowers known as catkins. These catkins are of two types, male and female. Plants of this family produce only male (staminate) flowers on one individual tree and only female (pistillate) flowers on another tree of the same species, and are called dioecious plants. Other plants, such as oaks, produce separate male and female flowers on the same tree and are called monoecious plants. The seeds of trees in the willow family are attached to extremely fine silklike or cottony hairs which permit the wind to carry them a considerable distance and thus provide for a wide distribution of these trees. The leaves of all members of this family are simple and are borne alternately on the twig. Since the leaves drop in the fall the trees are deciduous.

Poplars and willows are commonly found along stream beds, or in relatively moist places. To the early pioneers they were a welcome sight, since in most cases their presence indicated that water was near. They grow readily from root sprouts, seeds, or cuttings. In certain parts of the country it is not an uncommon sight to see a row of willows or poplars that are the remnants of an old fence line, having sprouted from green posts driven into the ground. Also, in the early days, willows and poplars were extensively planted as windbreaks, due primarily to the fact that they are extremely hardy and grew very rapidly. They also provided shade, fence posts, firewood, and some low-grade lumber.

Poplar (*Populus*)

In addition to the Aspen, Fremont Cottonwood, and Black Cottonwood discussed below, three other species of this genus are to be found in the Sierra Nevada. The Narrowleaf Cottonwood (*Populus angustifolia*), although quite common in the Rocky Mountain region has only been recorded in a few places in California, including Lone Pine Creek and Division Creek on the east side of the Sierra Nevada and Wyman Creek in the White Mountains.

Two introduced species have been widely planted in Sierran towns and on ranches. Lombardy Poplar (*Populus nigra* var. *italica*) is easily recognized by its slender columnar silhouette and is frequently seen in rows along ditches and roads. Silver Poplar (*Populus alba*) is readily identified as the cottonwood with the conspicuously white-tomentose undersurface of the 3- or 5-lobed dark green leaves. Locally these two species tend to escape and may become naturalized, particularly along streams and roads. Occasionally one of these trees will be found in a forest clearing where it has survived all signs of the original miner or settler who planted it.

Lombardy Poplar

Silver Poplar

Aspen (*Populus tremuloides*) Plate 6, *c*.

Also known as Quaking Aspen. This is a slender tree, 10 to 60 ft. tall, with a smooth greenish-white bark. Its leaf stalks are slender and flattened, allowing the leaves to flutter in the breeze, which accounts for its common name. The Aspen is responsible for much of the brilliant yellow coloration in the high, wet mountain meadows and slopes in the autumn and early winter. Aspens, with their white trunks and shimmering green leaves, are equally spectacular in summer. In winter the white trunks stand out in contrast to their usual green or gray background.

Leaves: Dull green on upper surface, paler on undersurface, 1 to 2 1/2 in. long and nearly as wide, broadly ovate with a short sharp point at the apex, margins finely or only slightly toothed. Leaf stem flattened.

Range: Widely distributed along stream banks, meadows, and damp slopes throughout the higher and cooler regions of North America, in the Sierra Nevada at 6,000 to 10,000 ft. April-June. Riparian Woodland, Sierra Mixed Coniferous Forest, High Sierra Subalpine Forest, bordering Mountain Meadows. Canadian Zone.

Fremont Cottonwood (*Populus fremontii*)

A handsome tree, 40 to 90 ft. tall, with a broad open crown. It is usually found along stream banks or beds and in moist places below 6,500 ft. Although the leaf stalk is flattened, it is somewhat thicker and heavier than the leaf stalk of the Aspen, and fluttering of the leaf blades is not as characteristic as with the Aspen. Its wood is fine-grained, soft, brittle, and has little commercial value except for fuel.

Leaves: Yellowish green on upper surface, lighter on undersurface, 1 1/2 to 3 1/2 in. long and as wide, broadly ovate, tending to be broadly heart-shaped or flattish at the base, tapering to a point at apex. Leaf stems 1 1/2 to 3 in. long, flattened, and yellowish.

Range: Moist places and along borders of streams in Sierra Nevada below 6,500 ft. April. Riparian Woodland, bordering Freshwater Marshes, Sierra Rural, Sierra Urban. Mainly Lower Sonoran Zone.

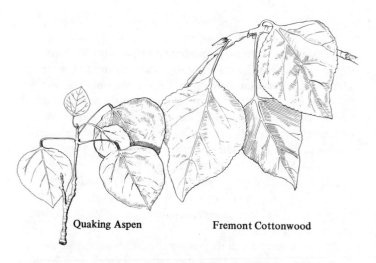

Quaking Aspen   Fremont Cottonwood

Black Cottonwood (*Populus trichocarpa*) Plate 6, *d.*

A big cottonwood, 40 to 150 ft. tall, with spreading branches forming a broad, open crown. Its grayish bark becomes darker and furrowed with age. The trunks of mature trees are usually free of branches for a considerable distance above the ground. The Black Cottonwood, like other poplars, prefers a moist habitat, hence it is frequently found along the banks of living streams or freshwater lakes. The wood is soft, straight-grained and has some limited commercial use. The poplar was most widely planted by the early settlers as a shade or windbreak tree in newly developed areas. Leaves vary considerably in size and shape depending on soil conditions, temperature, and moisture.

Leaves: Leaves variable, 2 1/2 to 5 in. long, 2 to 3 in. wide; shiny dark green above, much paler beneath; margins finely toothed, broadest near base, and pointed towards apex. Occasionally leaves may be less than 2 in. wide and somewhat lance-shaped. Leaf stalks 1 1/4 to 2 in. long, stout and rounded.

Range: Widely distributed in Sierra Nevada below 9,000 ft. February-April. Riparian Woodland. Upper Sonoran, Transition and Canadian Zones.

Willows (*Salix*)

There are numerous species and many varieties of willows in the Sierra Nevada, but only those that have definite treelike characteristics are treated in this book. Many species and varieties that are shrubby under certain conditions may be treelike in a more favorable environment. There is some disagreement as to which common name applies to certain species, and use of the scientific name will avoid confusion.

Red Willow (*Salix laevigata*) Plate 7, *a*.

Also known as Polished or Smooth Willow. A medium-sized tree, 15 to 40 ft. tall, native along streams where it is frequently associated with the Yellow Willow. It may be shrubby when growing under adverse conditions. The foliage at a distance appears grizzled when the wind turns up the whitish undersurface of the leaves. Bark of mature trees is usually dark and rough, while bark on young branches may be reddish brown.

Leaves and flowers: Leaves variable, 2 1/2 to 6 in. long, 3/4 to 1 1/8 in. wide, usually about 4 to 5 times as long as wide; rich green and shining above, glaucous on undersurface at maturity; margins only slightly toothed, lanceolate, and usually widest below the middle, although new leaves may be widest above the middle or near the tip, not long-tapering, rather thick and firm. Leaf stalk without glands. Catkins slender, 1 1/4 to 4 in. long.

Range: Sierra Nevada foothills along streams below 5,000 ft. March-May. Riparian Woodland, bordering Freshwater Marsh. Upper Sonoran and Transition Zones.

Yellow Willow (*Salix lasiandra*) Plate 7, *b*.

Also known as Golden or Red Willow. This is a graceful tree, 15 to 40 ft. tall, although it may sometimes appear shrubby. It is native along streams where it is frequently associated with the Red Willow. The bark of a mature tree is dark and rough with interlacing ridges. One-year-old branches tend to be yellowish.

Leaves and flowers: Leaves 3 to 6 in. long, 3/4 to 1 1/4 in.

wide, lanceolate, widest below middle and often long-tapering; dark green above, glaucous on undersurface at maturity; margins finely toothed. Leaf stalks 3/4 to 1 1/4 in. long with tiny bead-like glands near base of leaf; small glandular half-moon-shaped stipules at base of leaf stalk. Catkins stout, about 1 1/4 to 3 in. long.

Range: Widespread throughout Sierra Nevada on stream banks and moist places, below 8,000 ft. March-May. Riparian Woodland. Upper Sonoran and Transition Zones.

Black Willow *(Salix gooddingii)* Plate 7, c.

Also known as Gooddings Willow. A medium-sized willow, 20 to 40 ft. tall, sometimes shrubby. It is usually found along stream banks and wet places mostly below 2,000 ft. Trunks of mature trees tend to be dark and rough. Twigs tend to be yellowish.

Leaves and flowers: Leaves linear-lanceolate, 2 1/4 to 4 in. long and 1/4 in. or less wide, long, tapering, and rather thin; margins closely and finely toothed, tending to be grayish green on both surfaces. Young leaves usually pubescent. Leaf stalks 1/8 to 3/8 in. long, without glands. Catkins slender, 1 to 2 1/2 in long.

Range: Stream banks and wet places in Sierra Nevada below 2,000 ft. March-April. Riparian Woodland. Upper and Lower Sonoran Zones.

Arroyo Willow (*Salix lasiolepis*) Plate 7, d.

This is a small tree, 10 to 30 ft. tall, sometimes quite shrubby. Usually it is found on borders of flowing or summer-dry streams, or in arroyos. Bark of mature trees is dark gray. Twigs are yellowish to reddish brown and not widely diverging.

Leaves and flowers: Leaves oblanceolate, 2 1/2 to 5 in. long, 3/8 to 1 1/4 in. wide; dark green, and smooth above, hairy to smooth beneath; margins sometimes toothed and slightly rolled under. Catkins sessile, 1 1/4 to 2 1/2 in. long.

Range: Sierra Nevada stream banks and beds up to 4,000 ft. February-April. Riparian Woodland. Upper Sonoran and Transition Zones.

Nuttall Willow (*Salix scouleriana*) Plate 8, *a*.

Also known as Scouler Willow. This is a small tree, 10 to 30 ft. tall, sometimes shrubby. The bark on the trunks of mature trees is dull gray to blackish. Twigs are stoutish and vary from yellowish to brownish black. It is found along stream banks and in moist places up to an elevation of 10,000 ft. One of the most common willows in the Sierra Nevada.

Leaves and flowers: Leaves 1 1/2 to 3 1/2 in. long, 1/2 to 1 1/2 in. wide; variable in shape, usually widest above moddle, either very short-pointed or rounded at apex, thin; yellow-green and smooth above, silvery pubescent to smooth on paler under surface; margins entire or sometimes slightly toothed. Leaf stalks 1/4 to 1/2 in. long. Catkins 1 to 2 in. long and very showy.

Range: Along streams and in moist places in Sierra Nevada below 10,000 ft. April-June. Riparian Woodland. Transition and Canadian Zones.

Sandbar Willow (*Salix hindsiana*) Plate 8, *b*.

Sometimes known as Valley Willow or Gray Narrow Leaf Willow. A small tree, 10 to 20 ft. tall, frequently quite shrubby. The bark on mature trees is gray and furrowed. Bark on young twigs is gray and hairy. It is common along ditches, sandbars, river banks, and in flood beds.

Leaves and flowers: Leaves 1 3/4 to 3 1/2 in. long, 1/8 to 1/4 in. wide; linear, tapering at both ends; sometimes hairy on both surfaces, sometimes only on undersurface, sometimes not hairy at all but green and smooth. Leaf stalks 1/8 in. or less long. Catkins 1 to 1 1/2 in. long, tipped with short styles and long stigmas.

Range: Sierra Nevada foothills below 3,000 ft. March-May. Riparian Woodland. Upper and Lower Sonoran Zones.

Dusky Willow (*Salix melanopsis*)

A shrub or small tree, 9 to 15 ft. tall, branches widely divergent, twigs brown to blackish, often lustrous.

Leaves and flowers: Leaves 1 3/4 to 3 1/2 in. long; dark green and lustrous above, paler beneath; oblanceolate to elliptical, acute

61

Dusky Willow

at both ends, slightly and finely toothed; short stalked; stipules lance-shaped to somewhat heart-shaped. Catkins slender, appearing after leaves mature.

Range: Stream banks in Sierra Nevada below 8,000 ft. March-May. Riparian Woodland. Upper Sonoran and Transition Zones.

Mackenzie Willow (*Salix mackenziana*)

A shrub or small tree up to 18 ft. tall, branches dark brown, sometimes pubescent and somewhat yellowish when young.

Leaves and flowers: Leaves 2 1/2 to 4 1/2 in. long; dark green above, glaucous beneath; lanceolate to ovate lanceolate, tapering to short point at apex and rounded to somewhat heart-shaped at base, glandular-serrulate; stipules kidney-shaped to somewhat crescent-shaped. Catkins 1 to 2 in. long, appearing with the leaves.

Range: Sierra Nevada from Tulare County north at high elevations, 7,000 ft. Riparian Woodland. Transition and Canadian Zones.

Mackenzie Willow

WALNUT FAMILY (JUGLANDACEAE)

Hinds Black Walnut (*Juglans hindsii*)

This tree, unlike the shrublike Southern California Black Walnut, can reach heights of 75 ft. and diameters of 4 ft., its rounded crown supported by well-developed branches. Its bark is almost black and deeply furrowed; its wood is valuable for furniture, interior walls, and special uses involving the carver's skill.

Leaves and fruit: Leaves pinnately compound, 7 to 13 in. long with 11 or more serrate leaflets arranged alternately and decreasing in size from 5 to 2 1/2 in. long as they progress to the tip of the leaf. Fruit a spherical, thick-shelled, shallow-grooved nut about 1 in. in diameter which is surrounded with a green pulpy husk that dries to a black powder when mature.

Range: This is the only species of this family native to the Sierra Nevada and is found at the lowest elevations. For example trees are found below Placerville and north and south of Shingle Springs at elevations around 1,500 ft. and along Highway 49.

Hinds Black Walnut

April-May. Foothill Woodland, Sierra Rural, Sierra Urban. Upper Sonoran Zone.

BIRCH FAMILY (BETULACEAE)

There are two members (genera) of the Birch Family, namely Birch (*Betula*) and Alder (*Alnus*) found in the Sierra Nevada that normally attain tree size. Leaves of these cone-bearing broadleaf trees are deciduous, alternate and usually serrate. They have conspicuous straight and parallel side veins which extend from the midrib to the margin of the leaf. The small, unisexual flowers in catkins appear before or with the leaves. Male catkins pendulous, female catkins, erect or drooping, develop into small woody cones, which contain numerous small, flattened nutlike seeds. Cones of the alders are usually found in clusters and drop as entire cones while those of the Water Birch are solitary and disintegrate on the tree. When you find a mature cone-bearing broadleaf tree in the Sierra Nevada you know that it is either an Alder or a Birch. Alder cones, either sprayed or natural, make attractive Christmas decorations.

Birch (*Betula*)

Water Birch (*Betula occidentalis*) Plate 8, c.

Also known as Western Paper Birch. This is a tall deciduous shrub or small tree, 10 to 25 ft. tall. Bark, glossy reddish brown, smooth and not separating into thin layers. Twigs rough with large resinous glands.

Leaves and fruit: Leaves 1 1/2 to 2 1/2 in. long, usually more than half as wide as long; upper surface dull green, undersurface light green and minutely glandular; often in pairs but not opposite; ovate and broadly pointed, sharply and often double serrate except near base of leaf; parallel side veins. Solitary woody cones, 7/8 to 1 in. long, disintegrate on tree when ripe.

Range: Moist places at 2,000 to 8,000 ft. elevation, scattered locations in Inyo County and in White and Panamint Mountains; also, in southern Sierra Nevada. April-May. Riparian Woodland, bordering Sierran lakes and ponds. Transition Zone.

White Alder (*Alnus rhombifolia*)

This is a graceful deciduous tree, 30 to 100 ft. tall, usually with a straight trunk and spreading branches. Its whitish or grayish brown bark is characteristically broken into irregular plates on old trees. White Alders are frequently planted as park trees and, when sufficient space and moisture are available, develop into handsome specimens. The wood has limited use except as firewood.

Leaves and fruit: Leaves ovate, 2 to 4 in. long, 1 1/2 to 2 in. wide, often larger on new sprouts; dark green above, yellow-green and minutely hairy beneath; leaf margins finely to irregularly toothed to coarsely to doubly toothed; margins not rolled under, which helps to distinguish the White Alder from the Red Alder. Mature cones usually less than 3/4 in. long.

Range: River banks and canyon streams along the western slope of Sierra Nevada to an elevation of 7,000 ft. January-April. Riparian Woodland. Transition and Upper Sonoran Zones.

Mountain Alder (*Alnus tenuifolia*) Plate 8, *d.*

Mountain Alder is a deciduous shrub or small tree, 10 to 25 ft. tall, usually with a thin, bent trunk, especially when in dense thickets, larger trees may have a donelike crown composed of slim horizontal branches that droop a little. Bark is smooth and gray.

Leaves and fruit: Leaves 2 to 4 in. long, 1 1/4 to 2 1/2 in. wide, thin, ovate, acute at apex, rounded to heart-shaped at base,

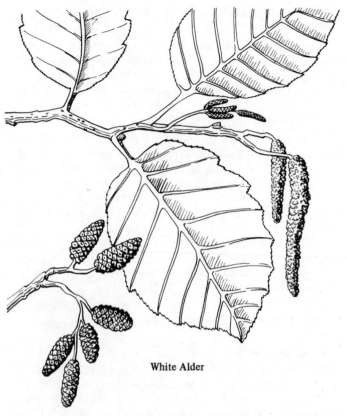

White Alder

conspicuous parallel side veins, upper surface dark green, under surface pale green and usually with orange midrib, regularly toothed. Cones 1/3 to 1/2 in. long, woody, usually in clusters, which drop as entire cones.

Range: Moist places in Sierra Nevada at 4,500 to 8,000 ft. elevation. April-June. Riparian Woodland, bordering Sierran lakes and ponds, Mountain Meadows. Transition and Canadian Zones.

BEECH FAMILY (FAGACEAE)

The Beech Family includes three members (genera), Chinquapin (*Castanopsis*), [3] Tanbark Oak (*Lithocarpus*), and Oak (*Quercus*).

Chinquapin (*Castanopsis*)

Giant Chinquapin (*Castanopsis chrysophylla*)

An evergreen tree, 50 to 150 ft. tall, with ascending or spreading branches forming a rounded crown. The Giant Chinquapin resembles somewhat the chestnuts of the eastern United States both in leaf form and fruit structure.

Leaves, flowers, and fruit: Leaves simple, alternate, 2 to 5 1/2 in. long, 1/2 to 1 1/2 in. wide; entire, oblong to oblong-lanceolate, thick, leathery; dark green above, golden-tomentose beneath becoming olive-yellow. Plants monoecious, both male and female catkins borne on the same tree. Fruit chestnutlike burs almost enclosing a shiny light-brown nut containing a reddish, sweet kernel.

Range: Scattered on western slope of Sierra Nevada in Eldorado County near Blodgett Forest. June-September. Yellow Pine Forest. Transition and Upper Sonoran Zones.

Tanbark Oak (*Lithocarpus densiflora*) Plate 9, z.

This is a broadleaf evergreen tree, 50 to 120 ft. tall with a thick gray-green and usually furrowed bark. Tanbark has long been an important source of tannin for use in the leather industry, although in recent years many other sources of tannin have been developed to supply the increased demand for this important material. Young branches are densely covered with short, soft hairs. This is not a true oak, but a near relative.

Leaves and fruit: Simple alternate leaves, 2 to 5 in. long 3/4 to 2 1/2 in. wide; oblong with blunt apex, prominent parallel side veins ending in sharp points; reddish-yellow new leaves covered

[3] Designated as *Chrysolepis* by some authors.

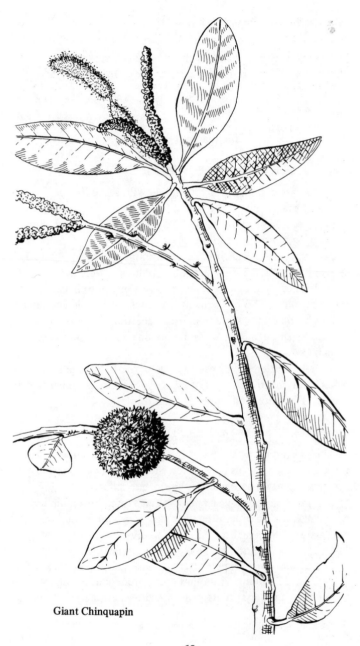

Giant Chinquapin

with a whitish or rusty fuzz which tends to disappear, leaving the upper surface smooth or nearly so. Ill-smelling erect catkins 2 1/2 to 4 in. long. Fruit an ovoid acorn, 3/4 to 1 in. long, with a shallow, bristly, saucer-shaped cup, maturing the second season.

Range: Western slope of Sierra Nevada below 4,500 ft. Foothill Woodland, Yellow Pine Forest. Upper Sonoran, Transition Zones.

Oak (*Quercus*)

The oaks are the most picturesque and widespread group of broadleaf trees in California. Some are small, trailing shrubs while others are large, spreading trees; some are deciduous and others are evergreen; some grow at sea level and others in the high mountains. The fruit of the oak is an acorn composed of two parts — a rounded, smooth-shelled nut, pointed at the outer end, and a scaly saucer or cup enclosing the base of the nut. The acorns of certain species furnished an important item of food for the early Indians. Six of the eleven California species classed as trees are found in Sierra Nevada.

Deciduous Oaks

Valley Oak (*Quercus lobata*) Plate 9, *b.*

Also known as Roble or California White Oak. A large, graceful, deciduous tree, 50 to 120 ft. tall, with wide-spreading and somewhat pendulous outer branches. Its thick dark gray bark is checkered and usually covered with light gray scales. Many fine specimens are being indiscriminately cut for firewood, a practice which should be discouraged in order to preserve this picturesque aspect of our landscape.

Leaves and fruit: Leaves 2 1/2 to 5 in. long, 2 to 4 in. wide; mainly oblong with 9 to 11 deep, rounded lobes, not spiny; upper surface dull green and finely pubescent, tending to become smooth as leaves mature, undersurface paler, pubescent, and yellow-veined. Acorns 1 1/4 to 2 in. long, 1/2 to 3/4 in. thick; cup deeply hemispherical with warty scales near base, maturing the first year.

Range: Western Foothills of Sierra Nevada, below 4,000 ft. March-April. Foothill Woodland. Upper Sonoran Zone.

Blue Oak (*Quercus douglasii*) Plate 9, *c.*

A medium-sized deciduous tree, 20 to 60 ft. tall with grayish, checked bark. Its short, stout branches tend to form a rounded crown. It is frequently associated with the Digger Pine.

Leaves and fruit: Leaves oblong to obovate, 1 1/2 to 4 in. long, 3/4 to 2 in. wide, shallowly and irregularly lobed or not lobed at all, smooth to minutely pubescent, bluish green above, paler underneath. Acorns commonly ovoid, 3/4 to 1 1/4 in. long; shallow cups with small warty scales, maturing the first year.

Range: Dry western slopes of Sierra Nevada below 4,000 ft. April-May. Foothill Woodland. Upper Sonoran Zone.

California Black Oak (*Quercus kelloggii*) Plate 9, *d.*

A deciduous oak, 30 to 80 ft. tall, its spreading branches forming a broad, rounded crown. Leaves on young shoots at higher elevations tend to be reddish in early spring. Leaves in the fall turn yellow to almost bright red producing a spectacular color effect when silhouetted against a varied and somewhat drab background.

Leaves and fruit: Leaves broadly elliptical to obovate, 4 to 7 in. long, 2 to 4 in. wide; lobes deep and sharp-pointed, each point tipped with a soft bristle; mature leaves smooth and dark green on upper surface, paler on undersurface; young leaves may be hairy or wooly on both surfaces. Acorns mature second year; cups wider than deep, slightly hairy on inner surface; nuts 1 to 1 1/2 in. long, cylindrical, rounded at apex.

Range: Common in Sierra Nevada, usually at elevations of 1,000 to 8,000 ft. April-May. Yellow Pine Forest. Transition Zone.

Canyon Live Oak (*Quercus chrysolepis*) Plate 10, *a.*

Also known as Maul Oak. Gold Cup Oak, or Iron Oak. This is a highly variable evergreen oak — it may be found growing as a small shrub on a high, dry exposure or as a massive tree, 60 to 70 ft. tall, in a moist canyon or open flat. Its sturdy, spreading, and somewhat irregular branches tend to form a widespread or, occasionally, a rounded crown. The wood is heavy, hard, tough, and strong. It was used by the early settlers for making mauls, wagon tongues, wheel stock, and parts of certain farm implements. Its characteristic leaves usually persist for 3 to 4 years. The bark of the mature tree is dark gray and scaly. Young twigs are usually covered with wooly hairs but they may be quite smooth.

Leaves and fruit: Leaves variable, usually oblong, 1 to 3 in. long, 1/2 to 1 1/2 in. wide; margins entire or toothed, stiff, leathery; bluish green above; underside of young leaves covered with a yellow powdery material: year-old leaves dull gray and smooth beneath; leaves on young vigorous sprouts quite spiny. Acorns oblong, ovoid, 1 to 1 1/4 in. long; cups more or less turban-shaped, first-season cups usually covered with a yellow powdery fuzz. Acorns mature the second season.

Range: Common in canyons and moist western slopes of Sierra Nevada, usually below 6,500 ft. April-May. Chaparral, Foothill Woodland, Yellow Pine Forest. Upper Sonoran and Transition Zones.

Interior Live Oak (*Quercus wislizenii*) Plate 10, *b.*

A beautiful evergreen tree, 25 to 75 ft. tall, with stout, spreading branches forming a rounded crown. In the San Jacinto Mountains and farther south it may appear quite shrubby. It has been used to a limited extent as a park or street tree; when sufficient space and care are provided it will develop into a handsome specimen. It, like the Coast-Live Oak, lends beauty and charm to the rolling foothills.

Leaves and fruit: Leaves 1 to 3 in. long, 3/4 to 1 3/4 in. wide; stiff, leathery, oblong, elliptical, ovate to lanceolate, entire to spiny, usually flattish; upper surface dark green, undersurface yel-

71

lowish green, smooth, no fuzz at junction of midrib and side veins. Acorns mature second season; cup turbanlike to cup-shaped; nut 1 to 1 1/2 in. long, slender, oblong and pointed.

Range: Western slopes and foothills of Sierra Nevada usually below 5,000 ft. March-May. Foothill Woodland, Foothill Chaparral, Yellow Pine Forest. Upper Sonoran and Transition Zones.

Oracle Oak (*Quercus morehus*) Plate 10, *c.*

A small evergreen tree, 20 to 40 ft. tall, which is sometimes quite shrubby. It is usually found near the California Black Oak and Interior Live Oak and is considered a hybrid of these species. Its acorns are quite similar to those of the Interior Live Oak, while its leaves are somewhat similar to those of the California Black Oak. Leaves persist until new leaves appear.

Leaves and fruit: Leaves 2 to 4 in. long, 1 to 2 in. wide; oblong to elliptical, with sharp, shallow, forward-pointing lobes tipped with a spine; dark green and smooth above, paler beneath. Acorns mature second season; cup turbanlike to cup-shaped; nut slender, 3/4 to 1 1/4 in. long.

Range: Scattered on slopes and foothills of Sierra Nevada below 4,000 ft., frequently near California Black and Interior Live Oak. Foothill Woodland, Yellow Pine Forest. Upper Sonoran and Transition Zones.

LAUREL FAMILY (LAURACEAE)

California Laurel (*Umbellularia californica*) Plate 10, *d.*

Also known in various localities as California Bay, Bay Laurel, Pepperwood, or Oregon Myrtle. This is an evergreen tree which may reach a height of 90 ft. or more in the northern part of the range or may be shrubby when found growing in dry places. Its ascending and spreading branches tend to form a broad, rounded crown when it is found in a relatively open stand. When crowded its crown may be open and irregular. Its crushed leaves emit a pungently aromatic odor suggesting camphor or bay, which serves as a positive identifying characteristic. Leaves are often used for flavor in cooking. The wood is heavy, hard, firm, fine-grained, rich yellowish brown, and frequently beautifully mottled. It is extensively used in the production of novelties and souvenirs such as plates, bowls, ash trays, figures, and the like. It is also used in the manufacture of some types of furniture. Since the wood is in such high demand and its supply is limited, serious consideration should be given to its most effective use, as well as to some satis-factory method of providing a continuous supply of this unique material.

Leaves, flowers, and fruit: Leaves 3 to 5 in. long, 3/4 to 1 1/2 in. wide; oblong-lanceolate or lanceolate; smooth, thick, leathery, and entire. Flowers in umbels. Fruit a yellowish green ovoid drupe, purplish when mature, about 1 in. long.

Range: Western slope of Sierra Nevada in canyons and valleys, usually below 6,000 ft. December-May. Foothill Woodland, Yel-low Pine Forest. Upper Sonoran and Transition Zones.

SYCAMORE FAMILY (PLATANACEAE)

Western Sycamore (*Platanus racemosa*)

Also known as Plane Tree. This is a large conspicuous, deci-deciduous tree, 40 to 90 ft. tall, often with stout twisted branches forming an irregular open crown. In open areas one will frequently find an old tree with large, heavy, and crooked branches which have developed near the ground, producing a chal-lenge to the venturesome tree-climbing boy as well as adding charm to the surroundings. Its dull brownish bark near the base is often quite furrowed and ridged, while a short distance above and on all branches it is smooth and ashy-white with greenish gray patches, which is a good identifying characteristic. It is com-monly found along stream beds and water courses in the drier areas of California, but not on the desert.

Leaves and fruit: Leaves 5 to 10 in. long, 6 to 12 in. broad, 3- to 5-lobed; mature leaves light green and tending to be smooth above, paler and usually rusty-hairy beneath; young leaves hairy on both surfaces, with conspicuous stipules at base of petioles. Fruit contained in bristly "button-balls," 3/4 to 1 1/4 in. in diameter.

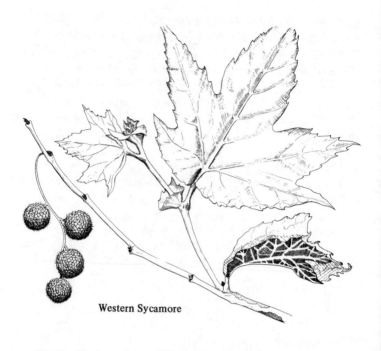

Western Sycamore

Range: Western slope of Sierra Nevada along stream beds and water courses. Usually below 4,000 ft. February-April. Riparian Woodland, Upper Sonoran Zone.

ROSE FAMILY (ROSACEAE)

Mountain Mahogany (*Cercocarpus ledifolius*)

Also known as Curl-leaf Mahogany. A small, evergreen tree or shrub, 6 to 25 ft. tall. Its short trunk is usually more or less crooked and its numerous stiff branches stand out in all directions producing a low, dense crown. It forms an important ground cover on dry windswept mountain slopes where few other species can survive. Its hard, dark, scaly bark is reddish brown with a grayish tint. Wood is brownish red and extremely hard. Due to the poor timber form of the tree, it has little value except for firewood and novelties.

Leaves and fruit: Leaves are thick and leathery, 1/2 to 1 in. long, 1/4 in. wide, edges somewhat rolled under; mature leaves dark green tending to be smooth above, paler and hairy beneath, margins entire, usually remaining on the tree for two seasons. Fruit is an achene with a long, hairy, and somewhat twisted tail.

Mountain Mahogany

Range: Eastern side of Sierra Nevada on dry slopes and washes at 4,000 to 10,000 ft. elevation. April-May. Foothill Chaparral, Foothill Woodland, Yellow Pine Forest. Transition and Canadian Zones.

Hard Tack (*Cercocarpus betuloides*) Plate 11, *a.*

Also known as Birch-leaf Mahogany. A small evergreen tree or shrub, 6 to 20 ft. tall, with more or less open and rounded crown. Bark on large trunks is thick, flaky, and reddish brown; on large branches and small trunks it is smooth and dull gray to brownish. Its habitat and value are similar to those of the Mountain Mahogany.

Leaves, flowers, and fruit: Leaves variable in shape, mostly obovate to oval, serrate above the middle, 1/2 to 1 1/2 in. long, 1/2 to 1 in. wide; dark green and smooth above, paler and frequently hairy beneath; straight parallel side veins. Flowers usually

75

in clusters of twos or threes. Fruit is an achene with long hairy
flower tube on tail.

Range: Dry slopes and washes below 6,000 ft. in Sierra
Nevada. March-May. Sagebrush-Shadscale Scrub, Pinyon-Juniper
Woodland. Upper Sonoran Zone.

Bitter Cherry (*Prunus emarginata*)

A small deciduous tree, 10 to 20 ft. tall, but it may also occur
as a shrub. Bark on mature trunks is smooth and dark brown.
Bitter Cherry tends to form dense chaparral cover on rocky and
dampish slopes and canyons, checking rapid runoff from heavy
snow packs. The wood has little value except for fuel. Its fruit
is eaten extensively by birds and many mammals.

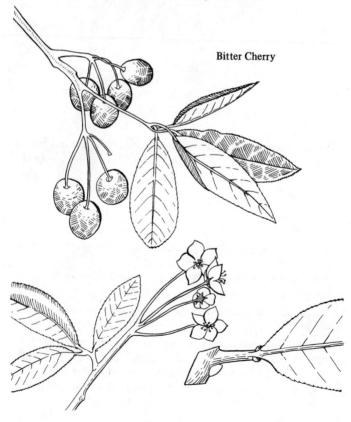

Bitter Cherry

Leaves, flowers, and fruit: Leaves oblong-ovate to broadly elliptic, acute to obtuse, 3/4 to 2 1/2 in. long, 1/2 to 1 in. wide, with 1 to 4 glands near the base of leaf, finely serrate; dark green and smooth above, paler and sometimes slightly pubescent beneath. Flowers in short clusters or 3 to 10. Fruit a drupe 1/3 to 1/2 in. in diameter, round, red, bitter.

Range: Widely distributed on mountain slopes and along stream banks in Sierra Nevada below 9,000 ft. April-May. Chaparral, Yellow Pine Forest, Sierra Mixed Coniferous Forest. Upper Sonoran and Transition Zones.

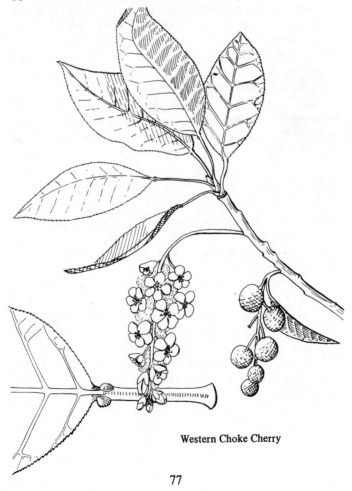

Western Choke Cherry

Western Choke Cherry (*Prunus virginiana*) var. *demissa*

A small deciduous tree or shrub, 6 to 20 ft. tall. New twigs are smooth or minutely hairy and greenish, turning light reddish brown, with pointed, light brown leaf buds. Bark on trunks of mature trees is grayish brown and somewhat scaly. Fruit is sweet when ripe but with an astringent aftertaste which probably accounts for the name "choke" cherry. It is frequently gathered and when cooked produces a rather delightful preserve. The fact that the fruit is greedily eaten by birds probably accounts for the wide distribution of this species.

Leaves, flowers, and fruit: Leaves oblong to oblong-obovate, 1 1/2 in. to 3 1/2 in. long, 3/4 to 1 3/4 in. wide; dark green and smooth above, slightly pubescent beneath; finely serrate, pointed at apex. One or two glands on leaf stalk near base of leaf. Flowers numerous, in racemes 3 to 6 in. long. Fruit a roundish drupe about 1/3 in. in diameter, dark red to purple when ripe.

Range: Widely distributed in Sierra Nevada on damp, brushy slopes and flats at elevations below 8,200 ft. May-June. Chaparral, Foothill Woodland, Yellow Pine Forest. Upper Sonoran and Transition Zones.

Sierra Plum (*Prunus subcordata*)

A small deciduous tree or shrub, up to 20 ft. tall, with stiff, crooked branches and somewhat spiny branchlets. Bark on old trunks grayish brown, becoming furrowed and divided into long thick plates. Young twigs reddish becoming purplish and finally ashen or brownish.

Leaves, flowers, and fruit: Leaves deciduous, ovate-elliptic to roundish, 1 to 2 in. long; finely toothed; dark green and glabrous above, paler beneath without glands. Flowers white in short clusters of 2 to 4. Fruit a drupe 3/4 to 1 in. long, red or yellowish when ripe.

Range: Sierra Nevada on rocky slopes from Kern County to Modoc County below 6,000 ft. March-May. Yellow Pine Forest. Transition Zone.

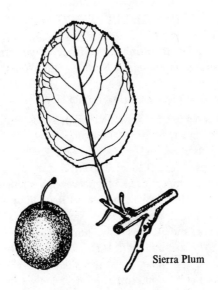

Sierra Plum

Toyon (*Heteromeles arbutifolia*) Plate 11, *b*.

Also known as Christmas Berry. A small evergreen tree or shrub 10 to 20 ft. tall, with a much-branched crown and a relatively short trunk. Its handsome green foliage and clusters of red berries lend much to the beauty of the California foothills in the autumn and early winter. Toyon is extensively cultivated as an ornamental, although the variety *macrocarpa*, a native of Santa Catalina and San Clemente Islands, appears to be more desirable as an ornamental since its flower clusters are larger and its berry-like fruit reputed to be less appealing to birds.

Leaves and fruit: Leaves thick, leathery, oblong to elliptical, 2 to 4 in. long, 1 to 1 3/4 in. wide, smooth and glossy; dark green above, paler beneath; tending to be pointed at both ends and rather sharply toothed. Fruit ovoid, 1/4 to 1/3 in. long, bright to pale red, berrylike.

Range: Common on brushy foothill slopes and canyons of the Sierra Nevada from Shasta County to Tulare County below 4,000 ft. June-July. Chaparral, Foothill Woodland. Upper Sonoran Zone.

PEA FAMILY (LEGUMINOSAE)

There is only one member of this very large family which reaches tree size in the Sierra Nevada — the Western Redbud.

Western Redbud (*Cercis occidentalis*) Plate 11, *c.*

Also known as California Redbud or Judas Tree. These are small deciduous trees, 8 to 15 ft. tall, whose dense rounded crowns nearly reach the ground, making them appear like small green clumps on the hillside. The striking, highly colored, pealike flowers, which appear before the leaves in umbellate clusters along the branches, make the Western Redbud one of the most attractive native flowering trees or shrubs. It is extensively culti-vated in parks and gardens throughout the West.

Leaves, flowers, and fruit: Leaves entire, smooth, glossy, almost round in outline, sometimes slightly notched at apex, heart-shaped at base and somewhat palmately veined. Flowers deep reddish pink to reddish purple, only rarely white. Fruit pods 1 1/2 to 3 in. long, turning dull red when mature.

Range: Dry slopes and canyons in Sierra Nevada below 4,000 ft. from Shasta County to Tulare County. Also, in inner Coast Ranges. February-April. Riparian Woodland, Foothill Chaparral, Foothill Woodland. Upper Sonoran Zone.

QUASSIA FAMILY (SIMARUBACEAE)

Tree of Heaven (*Ailanthus glandulosa*)

This tree is native to China and has become naturalized in the Sierra Nevada foothills along many of the streams and roads. Reports differ as to how it was originally introduced into Califor-nia. According to some authors it was brought by Chinese labor-ers when they came to work in the mines and on the railroads. It seems more likely that it was brought by early pioneers from New York and Pennsylvania where it was well established in the 1700s after introduction from England. It can be a slender deciduous tree, 30 to 70 ft. high, with few branches displaying a light green foliage with a disagreeable odor or shrublike in appearance with many suckers.

Tree of Heaven

Leaves, flowers, and fruit: Leaves to 3 ft. long, smooth, petioled, composed of 11 to 31 mostly opposite leaflets, each to 5 in. in length, pointed at the tip, with 1 to 4 blunt, glandular teeth at the base. Flowers small, greenish white, ill-scented. Fruit a samara or winged fruit about 1 1/2 in. long with the seed in the middle.

Range: Common in the foothills of the Mother Lode country along the streams and roads and in the towns. June-August. Riparian Woodland, Foothill Woodland, Sierra Rural, Sierra Urban. Upper Sonoran Zone.

CACAO FAMILY (STERCULIACEAE)

Flannel Bush (*Fremontodendron*)

There is only one species of these colorful plants which attains tree size in the Sierra Nevada. They are sometimes called "slippery elm" because of their mucilaginous bark and occasionally are also known as "silver oak" because of the light-colored under-surface of their leaves. However, they are commonly known in the nursery trade as Fremontia or Flannel Bush and are extensively cultivated in gardens and parks because of their long and showy blooming season. The showy part of the flower is the calyx, which consists of five petal-like sepals, each with a hairy gland at the base. They thrive best where there is good drainage.

California Flannel Bush (*Fremontodendron californica*)

A small evergreen tree or shrub, 10 to 20 ft. tall, with a short trunk and open crown of spreading branches. Frequently as a shrub it tends to form dense thickets with other foothill chaparral, producing a protective cover on dry, rocky foothill slopes. Range cattle and deer browse on its new twigs. It blooms more profusely and during a shorter time than the Mexican Flannel Bush.

Leaves, flowers, and fruit: Leaves simple, alternate, broadly round-ovate, usually 3- to 5-palmate, lobes rarely entire; dull green and sparsely star-shaped pubescent above, densely covered with tawny and matted woolly hairs beneath. Flowers consist of a flat, clear yellow calyx, 1 1/2 to 2 1/2 in. in diameter. Fruit is an ovoid capsule, 3/4 to 1 in. long, covered with dense bristly persistent hairs.

Range: The western side of the Sierra Nevada from southern Shasta County to Kern County on dry granite slopes below 6,000 ft. May-June. Pinyon-Juniper Woodland, Yellow Pine Forest, Chaparral. Upper Sonoran and Transition Zones.

California Flannel Bush

MAPLE FAMILY (ACERACEAE)

Three of the four maples that are native to California grow in the Sierra Nevada. There are a great many introduced varieties of maples in parks, on streets, and in gardens, many of which are very attractive and more desirable as ornamentals than the native varieties. All maples have opposite, deciduous, and simple-lobed leaves, except the Box Elder which has compound leaves. The fruit of all maples is a double samara with terminal wings.

Mountain Maple (*Acer glabrum* var. *diffusum*)

This is a small tree or shrub, 6 to 20 ft. tall, with grayish white twigs, in contrast to the Mountain Maple var. *torreyi* which usually has reddish twigs.

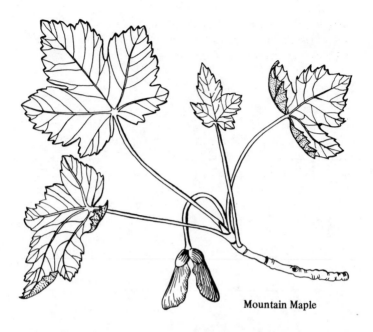

Mountain Maple

Leaves and fruit: Leaf blades smooth, shiny above and pale green beneath; 3/4 to 1 1/2 in. long, 3/4 to 2 in. wide; palmately three-lobed, occasionally with two supplementary lobes at the base.

Range: East slope of Sierra Nevada and on Panamint Mountains, Inyo-White Range at 6,500 to 9,000 ft. April-May. Yellow Pine Forest, Sierra Mixed Coniferous Forest, bordering Mountain Meadows. Canadian and Hudsonian Zones.

Mountain Maple (*Acer glabrum* var. *torreyi*)

A small tree or shrub 6 to 20 ft. tall, twigs slender and usually reddish.

Leaves and fruit: Leaves shiny green above, paler beneath; 1 to 2 in. long, 1 1/4 to 2 in. wide, slightly larger than leaves of var. *diffusum*; broadly heart-shaped at base, palmately three-lobed occasionally with two supplementary lobes at base. Fruit are samaras, about 1 in. long, usually extending away from each other at a 45° angle.

Range: Dry slopes and canyons of Sierra Nevada at 5,000 to 9,000 ft. April-May. Yellow Pine Forest, Sierra Mixed Coniferous Forest. Transition and Canadian Zones.

Big Leaf Maple *(Acer macrophyllum)*

Variously known as Oregon Maple, Canyon Maple, Water Maple, or White Maple. It is a tall, broad-crowned tree, 15 to 100 ft. tall, which may attain a trunk diameter of 12 to 20 in., occasionally shrubby in Sierra Nevada. Bark of mature trees is rough with hard, scaly ridges that vary in color from pale grayish to dull reddish brown. The wood is fine-grained, hard, firm, and of good commercial quality. It is an important lumber tree in certain parts of the Pacific area where hardwoods are scarce. It is easily recognized by its large 3- to 5-palmately-lobed leaves, which vary greatly in size depending on light, moisture, and soil conditions.

Big Leaf Maple

Leaves and fruit: Leaf blades vary from 6 to 18 in. long and as wide; shiny dark green above, paler and somewhat pubescent beneath; deeply-lobed, with lobes which may be 2- to 4-toothed or almost entire; petioles 6 to 12 in. long. Winged fruits or samaras vary in size, wings 1 to 2 inches long; early glabrous; seed body densely covered with short hairs.

Range: Widespread, in Sierra Nevada below 5,000 ft. on stream banks and canyons. April-May. Riparian Woodland, Foothill Woodland, Yellow Pine Forest. Mainly Transition Zone.

Box Elder (*Acer negundo*)

This is a fast-growing tree, 20 to 60 ft. tall, with a short clear trunk and a broad, roundish crown. Its bark is grayish brown with regular and deep furrows. New twigs are slender, greenish, and pubescent. It is the only native member of the maple family

Box Elder

that has compound leaves. The Box Elder was extensively planted by the early settlers to provide shade and windbreak. However, it has proven to be a rather undesirable domestic tree due to several objectionable characteristics: it is what some landscape designers call a "dirty" tree. It is brittle and frequently drops branches during a storm; its heavy crop of samaras drop over a long period of time; it serves as a host to the highly objectionable Box-elder Bug; and it drops its leaves early and continues to do so for months. The sap was reputedly used by the Indians and early settlers as a source of maple sugar.

Leaves and fruit: Leaves pinnately compound, 3 or rarely 5 leaflets, each leaflet more or less lobed or deeply serrate; 2 to 4 in. long; bright green and nearly smooth above, paler and pubescent beneath. Samaras abundant, usually finely pubescent.

Range: Sierra Nevada foothills below 6,000 ft. March-April. Riparian Woodlands, Foothill Woodland, Yellow Pine Forest. Upper Sonoran and Transition Zones.

BUCKTHORN FAMILY (RHAMNACEAE)

Cascara Sagrada (*Rhamnus purshiana*) Plate 11, *d.*

A small deciduous tree or shrub, up to 35 ft. tall. Bark smooth, grayish, used in drug manufacture. Young twigs thinly pubescent.

Leaves, flowers, and fruit: Leaves simple, tufted at the ends of branches, simple, alternate, oblong, elliptic, obtuse to rounded at apex, obtuse to somewhat heart-shaped at base, finely serrate; 2 1/2 to 6 in. long, 3/4 to 2 1/2 in. wide; dark green above, paler beneath, petioles 3/8 to 3/4 in. long. Flowers in umbels of less than 25 flowers, petals greenish white, notched at apex. Fruit spherical, black, berrylike drupe, 1/4 to 1/2 in. in diameter, mostly three-seeded.

Range: Sierra Nevada in moist places below 5,000 ft. from Placer County north. May-July. Yellow Pine Forest. Transition Zone.

BUCKEYE FAMILY (HIPPOCASTANACEAE)

California Buckeye (*Aesculus californica*)

Also known as Horse Chestnut or California Pear. A small deciduous tree, 15 to 30 ft. tall, with a broad round crown and smooth gray bark. It is one of California's most unusual and picturesque trees. In the late spring its profuse and beautiful, large, white flower clusters and lush green foliage are silhouetted against the dry and rolling foothills. With the advent of early summer drought its leaves begin to turn brown, and by midsummer the same hillsides are dotted with what look like dead or dying trees. Soon thereafter they lose their leaves and display their large pear-shaped fruit and shiny, smoky-gray branches until the early autumn rains start the cycle all over again.

Leaves, flowers, and fruit: Leaves dark green above, paler beneath; nearly smooth to finely pubescent; opposite; palmately compound with 5 to 7 oblong lanceolate serrate leaflets; 3 to 6 in. long, 1 1/2 to 2 in. wide. Flowers ill-scented, pinkish white with orange anthers in large erect cylindrical clusters, 6 to 10 in. long. Fruit a smooth, pear-shaped pod, usually containing one, sometimes two, glossy seeds, 1 to 3/4 in. in diameter; seeds bitter and slightly toxic.

Range: Widespread on dry slopes and in canyons of Sierra Nevada below 4,000 ft. from Shasta County south. May-June. Foothill Woodland. Upper Sonoran Zone.

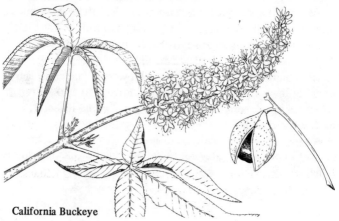

California Buckeye

DOGWOOD FAMILY (CORNACEAE)

Mountain Dogwood (*Cornus nuttallii*) Plate 12, *a*.

A small deciduous tree, 10 to 40 ft. tall, which varies greatly in form from a rounded to a narrow, long, open crown. Trunks are usually long and clean, with smooth, thin, ashy-brown or reddish bark. Young twigs vary from green to dark red. It is a spectacular native tree whose large white to pinkish flowers lend much beauty to mountain woods and meadows in the early spring. Its spring charm can only be surpassed by the brilliance of its autumn coloration, caused by clusters of bright red fruit and red and orange foliage.

Leaves, flowers, and fruit: Leaves are simple, opposite, deciduous, narrow, elliptic to obovate, or even ovate to almost round; 3 to 5 in. long, 1 1/2 to 3 in. wide; bright green and slightly hairy above, paler and pubescent to smooth beneath. Flowers small, yellowish green, crowded into a compact head, surrounded by usually six, sometimes four or five, conspicuous white bracts sometimes tinted with green or pink. Fruit a dense cluster of red to scarlet drupes about 1/2 in. long.

Range: Western slope of Sierra Nevada from Tulare County north below 6,000 ft. Also, in Coast Ranges. April-July. Riparian Woodland, Yellow Pine Forest. Transition Zone.

Miners Dogwood (*Cornus sessilis*)

A deciduous shrub or small tree, 5 to 12 ft. tall, with pale glabrous twigs becoming reddish-brown with age.

Leaves, flowers, and fruit: Leaves simple, opposite, acute, wedge-shaped at base, short petioles; 2 to 3 1/2 in. long, 1 to 1 1/2 in. wide; glabrous above or nearly so, paler and sparingly appressed pubescent beneath. Flowers in sparsely flowered axillary umbels surrounded by two pairs of deciduous bracts, petals yellowish. Fruit a drupe, whitish at first, then yellow to red and very dark.

Range: Sierra Nevada from Calaveras County north below 5,000 ft. March-April. Upper Sonoran and Transition Zones. Riparian Woodland, Yellow Pine Forest.

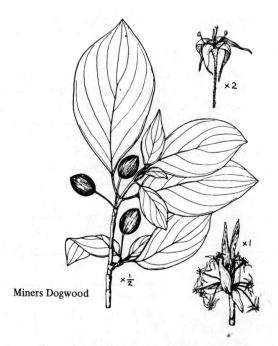

Miners Dogwood

HEATH FAMILY (ERICACEAE)

Madrone (*Arbutus menziesii*)

This is a handsome, wide-branched evergreen tree, 20 to 125 ft. tall (smaller in the southern part of its range), with a polished terra-cotta colored bark, which usually appears under a fully scaling dark brown and fissured older bark. The madrone is a picturesque tree that adds much beauty to the slightly humid hillsides and canyons. The attractiveness of the Madrone is due not only to the color of its bark and its beautiful, glossy, dark green leaves, but also to the large clusters of urn-shaped white flowers and brilliant orange-red berrylike fruits, which ripen in the late fall and make a very colorful display. It is quite extensively cultivated as a garden or park tree.

Leaves, flowers, and fruit: Leaves dark green and glossy above, paler beneath, thick and leathery, narrowly elliptic to somewhat

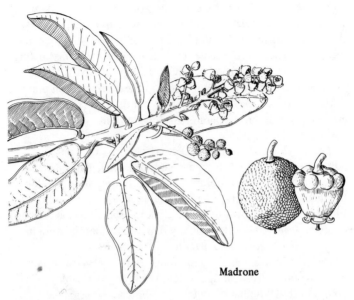

Madrone

ovate; 3 to 6 in. long, 1 3/4 to 2 3/4 in. wide; entire or finely serrate. Flowers urn-shaped, about 1/4 in. long, in large clusters, white to pinkish. Fruit 1/3 to 1/2 in. in diameter, somewhat fleshy, frequently abundant, deep orange to red.

Range: Foothills and mountain slopes below 5,000 ft. in the Sierra Nevada from Mariposa County to Shasta County. March-May. Yellow Pine Forest. Upper Sonoran and Transition Zones.

Parry Manzanita (*Arctostaphylos manzanita*)

Also known as Common Manzanita it is a small, picturesque evergreen tree or shrub, 6 to 20 ft. tall, without a basal burl and with long crooked branches. Bark is dark, smooth, reddish brown. Branchlets are minutely pubescent to nearly glabrous. It is the only manzanita among the many species found in the Sierra Nevada that frequently attains tree proportions, although others do so occasionally. The fruit of the manzanita, "little apples," which are really berrylike drupes, were very important in the diet of the early California Indians. Some authorities consider that the manzanita was as important a source of food for the early

91

Indians as the oaks or nut pines. The wood is extremely hard and was used by the Indians in making certain utensils and trinkets. In recent years the manzanita has been badly exploited by commercial agencies and souvenier hunters because of the fascinating asymmetry of its branches and the rich, skin-tight bark, which make it an attractive collector's item. Unless this wanton practice is discouraged we may eventually lose not only one of the picturesque aspects of our dry mountain slopes but also a very important erosion retardant.

Leaves, flowers, and fruit: Leaves bright to dull green, minutely pubescent when young, later becoming glabrous, stomates on both surfaces, oblong to broad elliptic, sharp-pointed to bluntish, thick and firm; 1 to 1 3/4 in. long, 3/4 to 1 1/4 in. wide. Flowers 1/4 in. long white to pale pink in drooping wide branched clusters. Fruit spherical or slightly depressed, smooth white in early summer, becoming a deep reddish brown.

Range: Foothills and dry mountain slopes of Sierra Nevada below 4,000 ft. from Mariposa County north. March-May. Chaparral, Foothill Woodland, Yellow Pine Forest. Upper Sonoran Zone.

Parry Manzanita

92

a. Lodgepole Pine
(Pinus murryana)

b. Western Yellow Pine
(Pinus ponderosa)

c. Jeffrey Pine
(Pinus jeffreyi)

d. Digger Pine
(Pinus sabiniana)

Plate 1

a. Knobcone Pine
(Pinus attenuata)

b. Sugar Pine
(Pinus lambertiana)

c. Bristlecone Pine
(Pinus aristata)

d. Foxtail Pine
(Pinus balfouriana)

Plate 2

a. Whitebark Pine
   (Pinus albicaulis)

b. Douglas Fir
   (Pseudotsuga menziesii)

c. Mountain Hemlock
   (Tsuga mertensiana)

d. White Fir
   (Abies concolor)

Plate 3

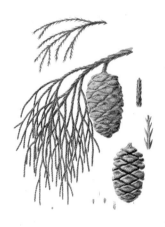

a. Red Fir
    (Abies magnifica)

b. Giant Sequoia
    (Sequoiadendron giganteum)

c. Incense Cedar
    (Calocedrus decurrens)

d. Macnab Cypress
    (Cupressus macnabiana)

Plate 4

a. Utah Juniper
(Juniperus osteosperma)

b. Western Yew
(Taxus brevifolia)

c. California Nutmeg
(Torreya californica)

Plate 5

a. Joshua Tree
   (Yucca brevifolia)

b. Mojave Yucca
   (Yucca schidigera)

c. Quaking Aspen
   (Populus tremuloides)

d. Black Cottonwood
   (Populus trichocarpa)

Plate 6

a. Red Willow
   (Salix laevigata)

b. Yellow Willow
   (Salix lasiandra)

ć. Black Willow
   (Salix gooddingii)

d. Arroyo Willow
   (Salix lasiolepis)

Plate 7

a. Nuttall Willow
(Salix scouleriana)

b. Sandbar Willow
(Salix hindsiana)

c. Water Birch
(Betula occidentalis)

d. Mountain Alder
(Alnus tenuifolia)

Plate 8

a. Tanbark Oak
   (Lithocarpus densiflora)

b. Valley Oak
   (Quercus lobata)

c. Blue Oak
   (Quercus douglasii)

d. California Black Oak
   (Quercus kelloggii)

Plate 9

a. Canyon Live Oak
   (Quercus chrysolepis)

b. Interior Live Oak
   (Quercus wislizenii)

c. Oracle Oak
   (Quercus morehus)

d. California Laurel
   (Umbellularia californica)

Plate 10

a. Hard Tack
  (Cercocarpus betuloides)

b. Toyon
  (Heteromeles arbutifolia)

c. Western Redbud
  (Cercis occidentalis)

d. Cascara Sagrada
  (Rhamnus purshiana)

Plate 11

a. Mountain Dogwood
    (Cornus nuttallii)

b. Dwarf Ash
    (Fraxinus anomala)

c. Oregon Ash
    (Fraxinus latifolia)

d. Blue Elderberry
    (Sambucus caerulea)

Plate 12

OLIVE FAMILY (OLEACEAE)

Ash (*Fraxinus*)

There are four members of the ash genus found in Sierra Nevada, all of which except the Oregon Ash are small trees or treelike shrubs. They have deciduous pinnately compound leaves except for the small Dwarf Ash whose leaves are usually simple, but occasionally trifoliolate. Fruit is a single-seeded samara.

Flowering Ash *(Fraxinus dipetala)*

Also known as Foothill Ash or Mountain Ash. A small deciduous tree or treelike shrub, 6 to 18 ft. tall, whose young branchlets tend to be 4-angled, slender, and somewhat pubescent. Older branches become smooth.

Leaves, flowers, and fruit: Leaves opposite, pinnately compound, 2 1/2 to 6 in. long, leaflets usually 3 to 9, thin, smooth on both surfaces, serrate, sometimes entire below middle, ovate to obovate; 1/2 to 1 1/2 in. long, 3/8 to 3/4 inches wide. Conspicuous part of flower consists of two showy, white petals. Fruit a single samara, 3/4 to 1 in. long, winged along the sides, often notched at the tip.

Range: Dry slopes, mostly below 3,500 ft. in Sierra Nevada foothills from Shasta County south. April-May. Chaparral, Foothill Woodland. Upper Sonoran Zone.

Arizona Ash (*Fraxinus velutina,* var. *coriacea*)

A small deciduous tree, 15 to 30 ft. tall, which usually has a rather short and slender trunk, with grayish, sometimes faintly reddish, soft and scaly bark. Crowns of the larger trees are dense and quite symmetrical. New branchlets are round, usually reddish and smooth, but sometimes dull grayish and occasionally covered with fine wooly hairs.

Leaves, flowers, and fruit: Leaves opposite, pinnately compound, 4 to 6 in. long; 3 to 7 leaflets, lanceolate to ovate, 1 to 1 1/2 in. long, thickish pale green and smooth above, paler and hairy beneath, finely serrate above the middle. Flowers greenish

Flowering Ash

94

Arizona Ash

without petals. Fruit a single samara, about 1 inch long, with terminal wing.

Range: Canyons and stream banks below 5,000 ft, desert mountain slopes north to Owens Lake. March-April. Riparian Woodland, Pinyon-Juniper Woodland. Upper Sonoran Zone.

Dwarf Ash (*Fraxinus anomala*) Plate 12, *b.*

Also known as Singleleaf Ash. A small, bushy deciduous tree or treelike shrub, 15 to 20 ft. tall. Its branchlets are smooth or somewhat hairy and tend to be 4-angled. Leaves usually reduced to a single leaf blade or leaflet, although it may sometimes have 3-pinnately compound leaflets. This characteristic helps to distinguish it from the Arizona Ash.

Leaves, flowers, and fruit: Leaves simple or pinnately compound; leaflets broadly ovate to almost round, 1 to 2 in. long, 1 to 2 in. wide; dark green and smooth above, paler beneath, entire or very slightly rounded serrate. Flowers greenish without petals. Fruit a samara, 1/2 to 3/4 in. long, with a rounded wing.

Range: Panamint Range and south above 3,000 ft. April-May. Pinon-Juniper Woodland. Upper Sonoran Zone.

Oregon Ash (*Fraxinus latifolia*) Plate 12, *c.*

A medium-size deciduous tree, 30 to 80 ft. tall, occasionally taller under ideal conditions. Bark on trunk dark gray or brown tinged with red. Branchlets stout, usually grayish pubescent until second season, then orange or light brown, becoming rough with large elevated leaf scars. Wood hard, valuable but not abundant. Trees in the open have beautiful compact broad crowns. They are used as shade trees in streets and dooryards.

Leaves, flowers, and fruit: Leaves 5 to 12 in. long; compound 5 to 7 leaflets, 3 to 6 in. long, 1 to 1 1/2 in. wide, terminal leaflet longer and stalked, lateral leaflets smaller; sessile or nearly so, ovate to elliptic, abruptly pointed; light green and nearly glabrous above, paler and usually pubescent beneath, entire or obscurely serrate above the middle. Plants dioecious, flowers without petals. Fruit a samara, 1 to 2 in. long, in crowded clusters, wings terminal.

Range: Western base of Sierra Nevada in moist canyons and near streams, below 5,500 ft., from Kern County to Modoc County. March-May. Riparian Woodland, Foothill Woodland, Yellow Pine Forest. Transition Zone.

HONEYSUCKLE FAMILY (CAPRIFOLIACEAE)

Elderberry (*Sambucus*)

There are three species of elderberries which attain tree size in California, only one of which, the Blue Elderberry, is found in the Sierra Nevada. The Red Elderberry is found in the Coast Ranges from San Mateo County north. The Mexican Elderberry, which is somewhat similar to the Blue Elderberry, is found in open flats and hills of the Sacramento and San Joaquin valleys, and in the coastal and interior valleys of southern California. The fruit of the elderberry is used in making drinks and preserves. The early California Indians called the elderberry the "tree of music" because they used it to make flutes, which were important instru-' ments in certain ceremonials. It also appears prominently in some of the early Indian mythology.

Blue Elderberry (*Sambucus caerulea*) Plate 12, *d*.

A small, deciduous tree or shrub, 20 ft. tall. Its branches have a large soft, pithy center. The bark of mature trunks is thin and dark yellowish brown. New twigs are usually smooth, sparsely hairy at first, then shiny reddish brown and somewhat angular.

Leaves, flowers, and fruit: Leaves opposite, pinnately compound, 5 to 7 in. long or even longer on new vigorous shoots; 5 to 9 leaflets, 1 to 4 in. long; oblong-lanceolate to ovate; smooth and yellow-green above, lighter and smooth to hairy beneath; serrate except near apex, sessile or very short-stalked; frequently with uneven base; lower leaflets occasionally pinnately divided. Flowers small, white, in flat-topped clusters, 4 to 8 in. wide. Fruit spherical about 1/4 in. in diameter, dark bluish with whitish bloom.

Range: Foothills, valleys and slopes of Sierra Nevada up to 8,000 ft. June-September. Riparian Woodland, Foothill Woodland, Yellow Pine Forest, Sierra Mixed Coniferous Forest. Transition and Canadian Zones.

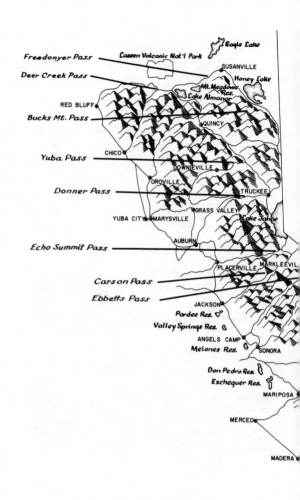

Freedonyer Pass
Lassen Volcanic Nat'l Park
Eagle Lake
SUSANVILLE
Deer Creek Pass
Honey Lake
Mt. Meadows Res.
Lake Almanor
RED BLUFF
Bucks Mt. Pass
QUINCY
Yuba Pass
CHICO
DOWNIEVILLE
OROVILLE
Donner Pass
TRUCKEE
GRASS VALLEY
YUBA CITY MARYSVILLE
Lake Tahoe
AUBURN
Echo Summit Pass
MARKLEEVIL
PLACERVILLE
Carson Pass
Ebbetts Pass
JACKSON
Pardee Res.
Valley Springs Res.
ANGELS CAMP
Melones Res.
SONORA
Don Pedro Res.
Exchequer Res.
MARIPOSA
MERCED
MADERA

MAP OF THE SIERRA NEVADA

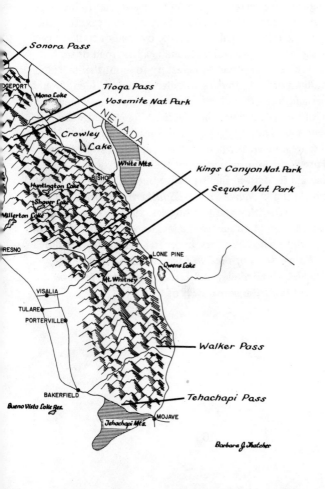

Sonora Pass

GEPORT

Mono Lake

Tioga Pass

Yosemite Nat. Park

NEVADA

Crowley
Lake

White Mts.

Kings Canyon Nat. Park

BISHOP

Sequoia Nat. Park

Huntington Lake

Shaver Lake

Millerton Lake

FRESNO

LONE PINE

Owens Lake

Mt. Whitney

VISALIA

TULARE

PORTERVILLE

Walker Pass

BAKERFIELD

Buena Vista Lake Res.

Tehachapi Pass

MOJAVE

Tehachapi Mts.

Barbara J. Thatcher

WHERE TO SEE TREES

One of the first problems confronting a person interested in identifying the various species of native trees is, "Where do I find them? " California is a large state that includes localities differing greatly in climatic and physiographic features, and specimens of a certain species of tree may be found in many places. However, once the identity of a species has been established, you will recognize it more readily each time you see it. Field trips to good tree-finding areas are recommended on the pages that follow with maps and species lists to guide you. Many of the areas are quite restricted, but are, in the main, accessible by road or trail. In general the designated species will be found near the road or trail. However, in some cases it will be necessary to scout the indicated area carefully in order to find a particular specimen. Identify all new species and recall those which have been previously identified, as repetition is extremely helpful in fixing recognizable characteristics in mind. Local park and forest rangers will be helpful in suggesting areas where certain species are to be found, as well as providing information about trail or road conditions.

A similar aid to assist in finding native trees of Southern California will be found in *Native Trees of Southern California,* by P. Victor Peterson (Berkeley and Los Angeles, 1966). That book covers the area from Monterey to the Mexican border, east to Arizona and north to where it meets, in general, the area covered by this book. *Native Trees of the San Francisco Bay Region,* by Woodbridge Metcalf (Berkeley and Los Angeles, 1959) will be helpful in identifying the native trees of that area.

LEGEND FOR MAP I, IA, AND II – VIII

— — — —	State Line
— · — · — · — ·	County Line
▬▬▬▬▬	Park Boundary
— ·· — ·· — ·· — ···	Streams
——————	Main Highways
—————	Secondary Highways
————— ┤ · · · · ·	End of Road, Trails Start
⊕	Ranger Station
△	Mountain, Peak
①	State Highway Marker
▯	U.S. Highway Marker

HIGHWAY 50 AND THE LAKE TAHOE AREA

MAP I

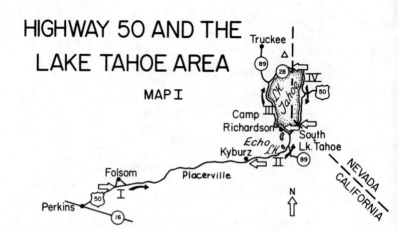

MAP I

NATIVE TREES FOUND ALONG HIGHWAY 50 AND IN THE LAKE TAHOE AREA

I. Highway 50 from the Folsom Junction to Kyburz:

Douglas Fir	Valley Oak
White Fir	Blue Oak
Incense Cedar	Canyon Live Oak
Digger Pine	California Black Oak
Western Yellow Pine	Interior Live Oak
Sugar Pine	California Buckeye
Western Sycamore	Mountain Dogwood
Bigleaf Maple	Toyon
White Alder	Yellow Willow
Black Cottonwood	Red Willow
Blue Elderberry	Arroyo Willow

II. Highway 50 from Kyburz to junction with Highway 89, including Echo Lakes, Highway 89 to Camp Richardson:

Incense Cedar	Aspen
Western Juniper	White Alder

White Fir
Red Fir
Western Yellow Pine
Jeffrey Pine
Lodgepole Pine
Sugar Pine
Western White Pine
Black Cottonwood

Canyon Live Oak
California Black Oak
Big Leaf Maple
Nuttal Willow
Yellow Willow
Arroyo Willow
Red Willow

III. Lake Tahoe Area. Highways 89 and 28 along west and north shores of Lake Tahoe from Camp Richardson to State Line north to South Lake Tahoe:

Incense Cedar
White Fir
Red Fir
Lodgepole Pine
Western Yellow Pine
Jeffrey Pine

Sugar Pine
White Alder
Black Cottonwood
Aspen
Yellow Willow
Nuttall Willow

IV. Lake Tahoe Area. Highways 28 and 50 along north and east shores of Lake Tahoe from State Line north to South Lake Tahoe:

Incense Cedar
White Fir
Red Fir
Lodgepole Pine
Western Yellow Pine
Jeffrey Pine

Sugar Pine
White Alder
Black Cottonwood
Aspen
Yellow Willow
Nuttall Willow

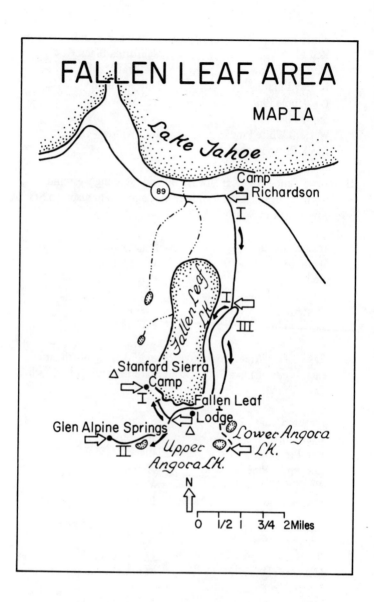

FALLEN LEAF AREA

MAPIA

Lake Tahoe

89

Camp
Richardson

I

Fallen Leaf Lk.

II

III

Stanford Sierra
Camp

I

Fallen Leaf
Lodge

Glen Alpine Springs

II

Lower Angora
Lk.

Upper
Angora Lk.

N

0   1/2 1   3/4 2 Miles

NATIVE TREES FOUND IN THE FALLEN LEAF AREA

I. Camp Richardson to Fallen Leaf Lodge to Stanford Sierra Camp:

Incense Cedar	Black Cottonwood
Western Juniper	Aspen
Douglas Fir	White Alder
White Fir	Mountain Alder
Red Fir	Mountain Maple
Giant Sequoia (planted)	Bitter Cherry
Lodgepole Pine	Blue Elderberry
Jeffrey Pine	Yellow Willow
Sugar Pine	Nuttall Willow

II. Road to Glen Alpine Springs from junction with road leading to Stanford Sierra Camp:

Incense Cedar	Black Cottonwood
Western Juniper	Aspen
White Fir	Mountain Alder
Red Fir	Bitter Cherry
Lodgepole Pine	Blue Elderberry
Western Yellow Pine	Yellow Willow
Jeffrey Pine	Nuttall Willow

III. Road to Angora Lakes from junction with road to Fallen Leaf Lodge:

Incense Cedar	Western White Pine
White Fir	Aspen
Red Fir	White Alder
Mountain Hemlock	Mountain Alder
Lodgepole Pine	Bitter Cherry
Western Yellow Pine	Yellow Willow
Jeffrey Pine	Nuttall Willow
Sugar Pine	Arroyo Willow

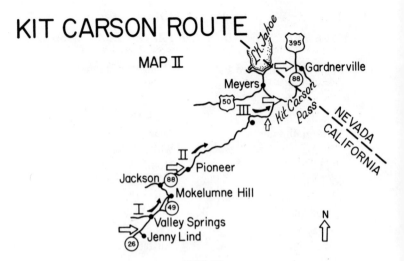

KIT CARSON ROUTE

MAP II

MAP II

NATIVE TREES FOUND ALONG THE KIT CARSON ROUTE

I. Highway 26 beginning six miles southwest of Valley Springs to Mokelumne Hill, Highway 49 to Jackson, Highway 88 to Pioneer:

Incense Cedar
White Fir
Douglas Fir
Western Yellow Pine
Sugar Pine
Digger Pine
Canyon Live Oak
Blue Oak
Interior Live Oak
California Black Oak
Valley Oak
Big Leaf Maple
Black Cottonwood

Fremont Cottonwood
Madrone
Bitter Cherry
Blue Elderberry
Mountain Dogwood
White Alder
California Buckeye
Toyon
Parry Manzanita
Yellow Willow
Red Willow
Arroyo Willow

II. Highway 88 from Pioneer to Kit Carson Pass:

Incense Cedar   California Black Oak
Western Juniper   Canyon Live Oak
Mountain Hemlock   Black Cottonwood
Red Fir   Aspen
White Fir   Big Leaf Maple
Lodgepole Pine   Bitter Cherry
Western Yellow Pine   Blue Elderberry
Jeffrey Pine   Red Willow
Sugar Pine   Yellow Willow
Western White Pine   Arroyo Willow
Whitebark Pine   Nuttall Willow

III. Highway 88 from Kit Carson Pass to junction with Highway 395:

Incense Cedar   Black Cottonwood
Western Juniper   Aspen
Mountain Hemlock   Bitter Cherry
White Fir   Elderberry
Red Fir   Mountain Mahogany
One Leaf Pinyon Pine   Mountain Alder
Lodgepole Pine   White Alder
Jeffrey Pine   Yellow Willow
Western Yellow Pine   Nuttall Willow
Western White Pine   Red Willow
Whitebark Pine

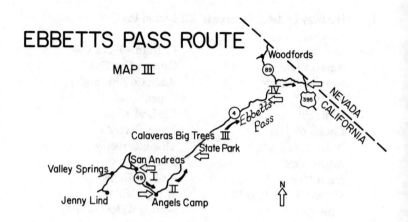

EBBETTS PASS ROUTE

MAP III

MAP III

NATIVE TREES FOUND ALONG EBBETTS PASS ROUTE

I. Highway 49 from San Andreas to Angels Camp:

Digger Pine   Fremont Cottonwood
Blue Oak   Black Cottonwood
Interior Live Oak   Yellow Willow
Valley Oak

II. Highway 4 from Angels Camp to Calaveras Big Tree State Park:

Incense Cedar   Interior Live Oak
Douglas Fir   California Black Oak
White Fir   White Alder
Giant Sequoia   Big Leaf Maple
Western Yellow Pine   California Buckeye
Digger Pine   Mountain Dogwood
Sugar Pine   Blue Elderberry
Blue Oak   Yellow Willow
Valley Oak   Red Willow

III. Highway 4 from Calaveras Big Tree State Park to Ebbetts Pass:

Incense Cedar	Lodgepole Pine
White Fir	Mountain Hemlock
Red Fir	Western Juniper
Giant Sequoia	California Black Oak
Western Yellow Pine	Aspen
Jeffrey Pine	Mountain Alder
Sugar Pine	Yellow Willow
Western White Pine	Nuttall Willow

IV. Highway 4 from Ebbetts Pass to junction with Highway 89. Highway 89 to junction with Highway 395:

White Fir	Bitter Cherry
Red Fir	Aspen
One Leaf Pinyon Pine	Black Cottonwood
Lodgepole Pine	Mountain Alder
Western White Pine	Mountain Mahogany
Jeffrey Pine	Yellow Willow
Mountain Hemlock	Nuttall Willow
Western Juniper	Blue Elderberry

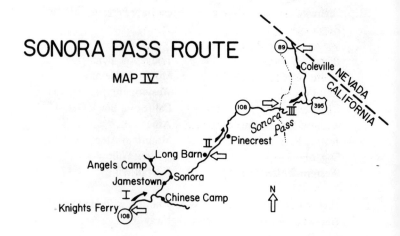

SONORA PASS ROUTE
MAP IV

MAP IV

NATIVE TREES FOUND ALONG SONORA PASS ROUTE

I.   Highway 108 from Knights Ferry to Long Barn:

Incense Cedar	California Black Oak
Western Yellow Pine	Fremont Cottonwood
White Fir	California Buckeye
Sugar Pine	White Alder
Digger Pine	Red Willow
Blue Oak	Arroyo Willow
Valley Oak	Yellow Willow
Interior Live Oak	

II.   Highway 108 from Long Barn to Sonora Pass:

Incense Cedar	Canyon Live Oak
White Fir	Black Cottonwood
Red Fir	Aspen
Western Juniper	Mountain Alder
Lodgepole Pine	Bitter Cherry
Western Yellow Pine	Blue Elderberry

Jeffrey Pine
Sugar Pine
Western White Pine
Whitebark Pine
California Black Oak

Parry Manzanita
Red Willow
Yellow Willow
Arroyo Willow

III. Highway 108 from Sonora Pass to junction with Highway 395; Highway 395 to junction with Highway 89:

One Leaf Pinyon Pine
Lodgepole Pine
Jeffrey Pine
Whitebark Pine
Western Juniper
Black Cottonwood

Aspen
Bitter Cherry
White Alder
Blue Elderberry
Yellow Willow

YOSEMITE NATIONAL

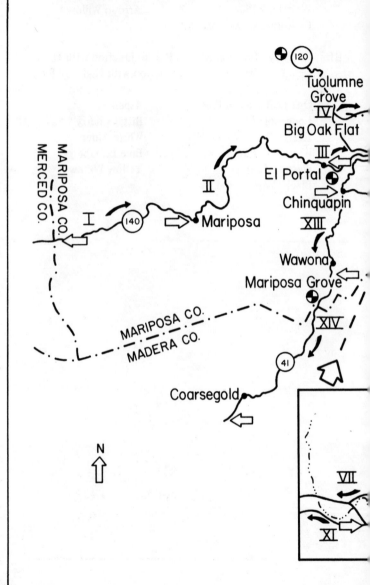

PARK AREA

MAP V

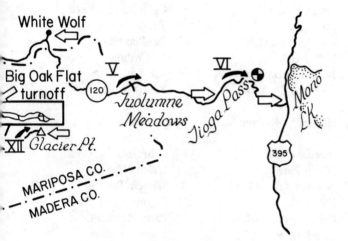

White Wolf

Big Oak Flat
turnoff

XII *Glacier Pt.*

120

Tuolumne Meadows

Tioga Pass

V

VI

Mono Lk.

395

MARIPOSA CO.

MADERA CO.

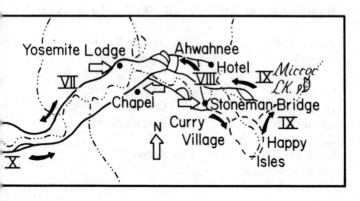

Yosemite Lodge

Ahwahnee
Hotel

Mirror Lk.

VII

VIII

IX

Chapel

Stoneman Bridge

Curry
Village

IX

N

Happy
Isles

X

MAP V

NATIVE TREES FOUND IN THE
YOSEMITE NATIONAL PARK AREA

I. Highway 140 from Mariposa County Line to Mariposa:

Digger Pine	California Buckeye
Blue Oak	Toyon
Interior Live Oak	Sandbar Willow
Valley Oak	Red Willow
Black Cottonwood	Arroyo Willow
Fremont Cottonwood	Yellow Willow

II. Highway 140 from Mariposa to El Portal:

Incense Cedar	California Buckeye
Digger Pine	White Alder
Western Yellow Pine	Western Red Bud
Blue Oak	Toyon
California Black Oak	Parry Manzanita
Interior Live Oak	Sandbar Willow
Canyon Live Oak	Red Willow
Valley Oak	Arroyo Willow
Black Cottonwood	Yellow Willow
Big Leaf Maple	

III. Highway 140 from El Portal to Big Oak Flat Road turnoff:

Incense Cedar	Western Red Bud
Digger Pine	Bigleaf Maple
Western Yellow Pine	Parry Manzanita
Douglas Fir	White Alder
Canyon Live Oak	California Nutmeg
California Black Oak	Blue Elderberry
California Buckeye	Yellow Willow
California Laurel	Arroyo Willow
Black Cottonwood	Red Willow

IV. Big Oak Flat Road to junction with Tioga Road; Tioga Road to White Wolf turnoff, including Tuolumne Grove:

Douglas Fir
White Fir
Red Fir
Giant Sequoia
Western Yellow Pine
Jeffrey Pine
Sugar Pine
Western White Pine
Lodgepole Pine
California Black Oak

Canyon Live Oak
California Laurel
Black Cottonwood
Big Leaf Maple
White Alder
Blue Elderberry
Bitter Cherry
Parry Manzanita
Red Willow
Yellow Willow

V. Tioga Road from White Wolf turnoff to Tioga Pass:

White Fir
Red Fir
Mountain Hemlock
Lodgepole Pine
Jeffrey Pine

Western White Pine
Western Juniper
Black Cottonwood
Aspen

VI. Tioga Road from Tioga Pass to junction with Highway 395:

Western Juniper
One Leaf Pinyon Pine
Lodgepole Pine
Whitebark Pine
Jeffrey Pine

Black Cottonwood
Aspen
Mountain Mahogany
Yellow Willow
Nuttall Willow

VII. Northside Drive from Yosemite Lodge to Big Oak Flat turnoff:

Incense Cedar
Douglas Fir
White Fir
Western Yellow Pine

California Laurel
Black Cottonwood
Western Choke Cherry
Red Willow

Canyon Live Oak
California Black Oak
White Alder
Big Leaf Maple

Yellow Willow
Nuttall Willow
Mountain Dogwood

VIII. Road from Yosemite Lodge to Stoneman Bridge including Ahwahnee Hotel grounds:

Incense Cedar
Douglas Fir
Western Yellow Pine
Giant Sequoia (planted,
  Ahwahnee Hotel grounds)
California Black Oak
Canyon Live Oak

Mountain Dogwood
Aspen
White Alder
Western Redbud (planted,
  Ahwahnee Hotel grounds)
California Laurel
Big Leaf Maple

IX. Road from Stoneman Bridge to Happy Isles to Mirror Lake:

Incense Cedar
White Fir
Douglas Fir
Lodgepole Pine
Western Yellow Pine
Sugar Pine
California Black Oak
Canyon Live Oak

California Laurel
Black Cottonwood
Big Leaf Maple
Blue Elderberry
Mountain Dogwood
White Alder
Yellow Willow
Red Willow

X. Southside Drive from Chapel Area to Merced Road turnoff:

Incense Cedar
White Fir
Red Fir
Douglas Fir
Western Yellow Pine
Lodgepole Pine
Giant Sequoia (planted
  near Chapel)
Canyon Live Oak

California Black Oak
California Laurel
Big Leaf Maple
Black Cottonwood
Western Choke Cherry
Red Willow
Yellow Willow

XI. South Valley Road from Merced Road turnoff, through tunnel to Chinquapin:

Incense Cedar	Canyon Live Oak
Douglas Fir	White Alder
White Fir	Big Leaf Maple
Red Fir	California Laurel
California Nutmeg	Blue Elderberry
Western Yellow Pine	Parry Manzanita
Sugar Pine	Red Willow
California Black Oak	

XII. Glacier Point Road from Chinquapin to Glacier Point:

Incense Cedar	Sugar Pine
White Fir	Western White Pine
Red Fir	California Black Oak
Douglas Fir	Aspen
Western Yellow Pine	Blue Elderberry
Lodgepole Pine	Bitter Cherry
Jeffrey Pine	Yellow Willow

XIII. Road from Chinquapin to Checking Station, South Entrance, including Mariposa Grove:

Incense Cedar	Canyon Live Oak
White Fir	Mountain Alder
Red Fir	Parry Manzanita
Douglas Fir	Mountain Mahogany
Giant Sequoia	Blue Elderberry
Yellow Pine	Yellow Willow
Sugar Pine	Arroyo Willow
California Black Oak	Mountain Dogwood

XIV. Highway 41 from South Entrance to 10 miles south of Coarsegold:

Incense Cedar
White Fir
Yellow Pine
Digger Pine
Sugar Pine
California Black Oak
Blue Oak
Interior Live Oak
Valley Oak
Canyon Live Oak

Fremont Cottonwood
Black Cottonwood
Aspen
White Alder
California Buckeye
Parry Manzanita
California Laurel
Red Willow
Arroyo Willow
Yellow Willow

MAP VI

NATIVE TREES FOUND IN THE MAMMOTH LAKES AREA

I. Roads including Highway 203, Old Mammoth Road and Mammoth Creek Road to Twin Lakes, from junctions, with Highway 395:

White Fir
Red Fir
One Leaf Pinyon Pine
Lodgepole Pine
Jeffrey Pine
Limber Pine

Utah Juniper
Western Juniper
Mountain Alder
Black Cottonwood
Aspen
Yellow Willow
Nuttall Willow

II. Mammoth Lake Area — Twin Lakes, Lake Mary, Lake George, Lake Mamie, Horseshoe Lake:

Red Fir
Lodgepole Pine
Jeffrey Pine
Western White Pine
Mountain Hemlock

Aspen
Mountain Alder
Bitter Cherry
Yellow Willow
Nuttall Willow

118

MAMMOTH LAKES AREA

MAP VI

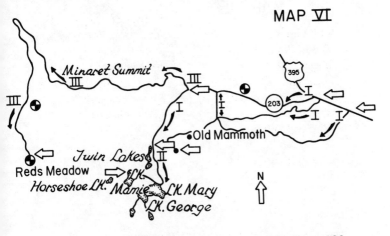

III.   Road to Reds Meadow from junction with Highway 203 including Minaret Summit:

White Fir   Mountain Hemlock
Red Fir   Aspen
Lodgepole Pine   Black Cottonwood
Jeffrey Pine   Blue Elderberry
Western White Pine   Mountain Alder
White Bark Pine   Yellow Willow

HUNTINGTON LAKE AREA
MAP VII

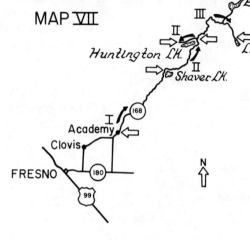

Edison LK.

Lk. Florence

Huntington LK.

Shaver LK.

168

Academy

Clovis

FRESNO

180

99

N

MAP VII

NATIVE TREES FOUND IN THE
HUNTINGTON LAKE AREA

I. Highway 168 from Academy to Shaver Lake:

Incense Cedar
White Fir
Digger Pine
Western Yellow Pine
Jeffrey Pine
Sugar Pine
Valley Oak
California Black Oak
Blue Oak
Interior Live Oak
Canyon Live Oak
Fremont Cottonwood

Black Cottonwood
Western Sycamore
California Buckeye
Western Red Bud
Parry Manzanita
California Laurel
White Alder
Blue Elderberry
Bitter Cherry
Yellow Willow
Red Willow
Arroyo Willow

II. Highway 168 from Shaver Lake to Huntington Lake:

Incense Cedar   California Black Oak
White Fir   Canyon Live Oak
Red Fir   Blue Elderberry
Western Yellow Pine   Bitter Cherry
Jeffrey Pine   White Alder
Sugar Pine   Parry Manzanita
Lodgepole Pine   Yellow Willow
Western Juniper   Nuttall Willow

III. Road from Huntington Lake to Florence Lake:

Incense Cedar   Aspen
White Fir   Black Cottonwood
Red Fir   California Black Oak
Western Juniper   Mountain Alder
Lodgepole Pine   Bitter Cherry
Jeffrey Pine   Blue Elderberry
Sugar Pine   Yellow Willow
Western White Pine   Nuttall Willow
Whitebark Pine

SEQUOIA AND KINGS CANYON NATIONAL PARK AREA

MAP VIII

MAP VIII

NATIVE TREES FOUND IN THE
SEQUOIA AND KINGS CANYON NATIONAL PARKS AREA

I. Highway 180 from Squaw Valley to General Grant Grove:

      Incense Cedar   Fremont Cottonwood
      White Fir   California Laurel
      Red Fir   Bitter Cherry

Giant Sequoia
Western Yellow Pine
Jeffrey Pine
Sugar Pine
Blue Oak
California Black Oak
Interior Live Oak
Canyon Live Oak
Western Sycamore

Western Redbud
California Buckeye
Blue Elderberry
Parry Manzanita
Mountain Mahogany
Red Willow
Arroyo Willow
Yellow Willow

II.   Road from General Grant Grove to Boyden Caves:

Incense Cedar
White Fir
Red Fir
Giant Sequoia
Western Yellow Pine
Jeffrey Pine
Sugar Pine
California Nutmeg
Red Bud
Fremont Cottonwood
Black Cottonwood
Bitter Cherry

Big Leaf Maple
California Laurel
California Buckeye
Canyon Live Oak
Interior Live Oak
California Black Oak
Blue Elderberry
Parry Manzanita
Mountain Mahogany
Yellow Willow
Nuttall Willow
Red Willow

III.   Road from Boyden Caves to Zumwalt Meadow:

Incense Cedar
White Fir
Western Juniper
One Leaf Pinon Pine
Western Yellow Pine
Sugar Pine
Giant Sequoia (planted,
   Ranger Headquarters)
California Nutmeg
Canyon Live Oak
California Black Oak
Black Cottonwood

Big Leaf Maple
California Laurel
Western Red Bud
California Buckeye
White Alder
Blue Elderberry
Parry Manzanita
Arroyo Willow
Red Willow
Yellow Willow

IV.   Road from General Grant Grove to Lodgepole:

Incense Cedar
Sierra Juniper (Stillman
  Creek)
Giant Sequoia
White Fir
Red Fir
Western Yellow Pine
Lodgepole Pine
Jeffrey Pine
Sugar Pine
Western White Pine

Canyon Live Oak
California Black Oak
Aspen
Black Cottonwood
Bitter Cherry
Blue Elderberry
Nuttall Willow
Arroyo Willow

V.   Road from Lodgepole to Camp Kaweah, including Lodgepole and Wolverton Areas:

Incense Cedar
Giant Sequoia
White Fir
Red Fir
Lodgepole Pine
Sugar Pine
Western White Pine

Jeffrey Pine
California Black Oak
Aspen
Black Cottonwood
Mountain Dogwood
Blue Elderberry
Yellow Willow

VI.   Road from Camp Kaweah to Moro Rock, Crescent Meadow
and surrounding areas:

Incense Cedar
Giant Sequoia
White Fir
Red Fir
California Nutmeg
  (Moro Rock Area)
Yellow Pine
Jeffrey Pine
Sugar Pine

Canyon Live Oak
California Black Oak
Aspen
Mountain Dogwood
Arroyo Willow
Nuttall Willow
Yellow Willow

VII. Road from Camp Kaweah to Ash Mountain:

Incense Cedar
Giant Sequoia
White Fir
Yellow Pine
Jeffrey Pine
Sugar Pine
Canyon Live Oak
California Black Oak
Blue Oak
Interior Live Oak
White Alder

California Laurel
Big Leaf Maple
California Buckeye
Western Redbud
Blue Elderberry
Mountain Dogwood
Fremont Cottonwood
Western Sycamore
Parry Manzanita
Yellow Willow

VIII. Highway 198 from Ash Mountain to Lake Kaweah:

Western Yellow Pine
Valley Oak
Interior Live Oak
California Black Oak
Blue Oak
California Laurel
Western Sycamore

Western Redbud
Parry Manzanita
California Buckeye
Fremont Cottonwood
Sandbar Willow
Red Willow
Arroyo Willow

PRIVATELY ENDOWED BOTANIC GARDENS

In California there are two excellent privately endowed and supported botanic gardens devoted to the propagation and study of native and hybridized California plants. Both gardens are open to the public.

The Rancho Santa Ana Botanic Garden was founded in 1927 by Susanna Bixby Bryant in the rolling foothills in the Santa Ana Canyon area. In 1948 it was relocated on an eighty-acre site at 1500 North College Avenue in Claremont about a third of a mile north of Foothill Boulevard (U.S. Highway 66). Except for some magnificent Coast Live Oaks, most of the trees in the garden have been planted since 1948, hence they exhibit for the most part the characteristics of the immature tree. However, many specimens do display the major features that these species assume in a semi-protected environment. Most of the trees described in this book are found in the garden. In addition to native trees, the garden has an extensive collection of native shrubs, herbs, desert, and sea-shore plants, as well as a home demonstration garden showing the landscape use of native plants.

The Santa Barbara Botanic Garden, located at 1212 Mission Canyon Road in Santa Barbara, was established in 1926 at the instigation of a small group of citizens interested in the preservation and study of the native flora of California. Mrs. Anna Blaksley Bliss purchased the first fifteen acres in the memory of her father, Henry J. Blaksley, for whom the garden was originally named. More land has been added from time to time so that it now contains fifty acres. In 1939 the name was changed to Santa Barbara Botanic Garden. Most of the trees found in the garden are quite mature and exhibit in general the characteristics shown by these species when they are grown in a somewhat protected environment. Many native trees of the Sierra Nevada can be found in this well-designed garden. It also contains an extensive collection of shrubs, herbs, and other plants. Special attention has been focused on the use of native plants in home gardens.

Two other gardens worth visiting are the Tilden Park Botanic Garden in the Berkeley hills and the Strybing-Arboretum in Golden Gate Park in San Francisco.

ACTIVITIES

MAKE AN AREA TREE MAP

When you travel about the state, either by road or trail, secure or make a map of the area. Name and locate on it the various species of trees that you see. Take silhouette pictures of a typical specimen of each species, and, if possible, take colored pictures of its fruit, leaves, and bark. File these with the map for future review and reference.

MAKE AN HERBARIUM

You may wish to make an herbarium including the species which you have identified and located on your tree map. If so, collect typical leaves, flowers (if available), fruit, twigs showing buds (if possible), and bark. Place the leaves, flowers, and twigs between heavy layers of newspapers or blotters to dry, being careful to place specimens so that they do not overlap each other. Several separate specimen-containing layers may be laid on top of each other and the entire package placed between two pieces of uniformly weighted plywood or heavy cardboard. (If you plan an extensive herbarium you may wish to make or buy an herbarium press.) When specimens are thoroughly dry they should be mounted with special herbarium tape or herbarium glue on heavy stiff paper on which should be noted the name of the species, location, and date of collection. Each paper should be filed separately in a manila folder and stored in a closed container. Large cones, when properly labeled, may be kept on shelves or in open containers. Small cones, acorns, bark, and some small dried fruits may be conveniently stored and displayed in discarded cellophane-topped Christmas card boxes. In some cases you may wish to place the specimens on a pad of cotton in order to hold them in place and near the top of the container.

Permanently mounted specimens that have been correctly identified will prove very helpful in identifying new material.

HERBARIUM SHEET

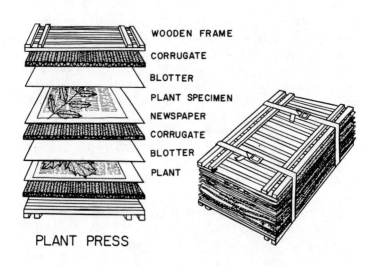

WOODEN FRAME
CORRUGATE
BLOTTER
PLANT SPECIMEN
NEWSPAPER
CORRUGATE
BLOTTER
PLANT

PLANT PRESS

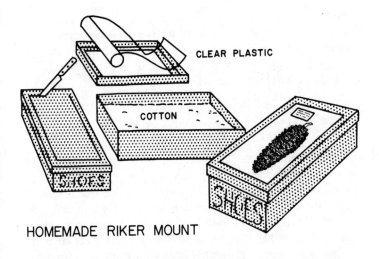

CLEAR PLASTIC

COTTON

SHOES

SHOES

HOMEMADE RIKER MOUNT

MAKE A CHECK LIST OF LOCAL NATIVE TREES

Make a check list of the native trees found in your community. Indicate on a map the specific location of each species. Which of these trees was planted by man? Compare the growth pattern of native trees planted in public parks and home ground with those of the same species found in their native habitat. Account for the variations which you may observe. You may wish to take silhouette pictures and also to make an herbarium collection of specimens from native cultivated trees for comparative purposes.

AGE OF TREES

Examine the cross-section of a log cut from near the base of the tree and note the concentric rings that start at or near the center and extend to the perimeter of the log. Each ring represents the growth of one year. Smooth the cut surface with sandpaper and carefully count the rings to determine the age of the tree. You may need a hand lens or a powerful reading glass in order to make an accurate count. Often the stump of an old tree shows the rings quite distinctly. If so, smooth the surface and make a count. Recount to verify your estimate. Tree rings are used to determine the age of such very old trees as redwoods, cypresses, and junipers. Slender core borings are used to determine the age of standing trees. The size and character of tree rings tell us a great deal about past climatic conditions.

MAKE AND STUDY A WOOD COLLECTION

Contact some of the lumber companies in your neighborhood to see if you can secure from or through them display samples of woods representing the various native trees of the Sierra Nevada. Unless the samples have already been prepared for display, smooth all surfaces with fine sandpaper and examine each carefully with a hand lens, noting similarities and differences in both surface and end-grain patterns. End-grain patterns are very distinctive and provide a positive means of wood identification. Study each sample carefully until you can recognize the same wood when found in a piece of furniture or in a building which is under construction. You may wish to extend your observations to include all of the common commercial woods, irrespective of their source. Make a list of the woods commonly used in furniture and house construction.

ENEMIES OF THE FOREST

Fire, insects, and disease are common enemies of the forest. Which of these do you think accounts for the greatest financial losses? (Check your estimates with government statistics.) What methods are being used to combat the ravages of each and with what success? What secondary damages occur as a result of each?

Fire and insects can also be considered beneficial to the forest. Investigate current thought on the role of fire in the ecology of the forest. In what way could insects be beneficial in the forest?

WOOD PRODUCTS

Prepare a list of products derived directly or indirectly from trees. Check your library and various commercial publications for source material. List some products which twenty years ago were derived almost exclusively from trees which are now derived principally from other sources. Account for this change.

MAKE A LAND UTILIZATION STUDY

Make a study of the land utilization of the United States, noting the percentage of the national land mass in each of the following categories: 1. forests, (a) public, (b) private; 2. agriculture, (a) cultivation, (b) grazing; 3. nonproductive, (a) deserts, (b) barren mountains, (c) swamps and submerged areas. You may wish to study further the type of products produced in the various public and private forests, the extent and success of reforestation, and recovery of nonproductive lands through irrigation and drainage. You may wish to record your findings on a map.

LIFE IN FOREST ENVIRONS

Select a deep forest as a starting point. Note the size and type of trees; the undergrowth, including the smaller annuals; and the animals which inhabit the area. The latter should include the birds, mammals, reptiles, amphibia, and insects. Now proceed towards the edge of the forest and finally into the open meadow. Note the changes in the plant and animal life as you move from one environment to another. Try to account for these changes. This project will take several days since you will need to spend at least an entire day in each of the different areas and some time for rechecking. Why do you suppose that the animals distribute themselves as they do? Why are the leaves of certain plants larger in the forest than in the open meadow? Why do the trees develop a different silhouette in the deep forest than in the open areas? These and dozens of other questions will come to mind as you work with this project, which you may wish to combine with a summer camp trip.

STUDY FOREST RECOVERY IN BURNED AREAS

Select several forest areas for study. In order to have a good basis for comparison you will need to examine some areas which were burned fifteen or twenty years ago and compare these with areas which have been burned recently. List in order of appearance the type of vegetation, including brush and trees, that follows a devastating fire in an open forest and in a dense forest. Note the change in animal habitation in such areas. Note the erosion effects in a denuded area. What are some of the more remote effects of such a catastrophe? List cautions which must be observed to prevent destructive forest fires. What measures can be taken to hasten restoration and to minimize erosion in burned areas?

MAKE A SURVEY OF THE CALIFORNIA PUBLIC RECREATIONAL FACILITIES

Secure from the various local, state, and federal agencies maps showing the location of such recreational areas under their jurisdiction as community, city, county, and state parks and beaches and national parks, monuments, and forests. You may wish to locate those areas which lie within California on a single map. You will be impressed with the number and extent of publicly owned and controlled reserves. Visit as many of these areas as possible and make notes concerning the following: (a) factors which caused the area to be set aside as a public reserve; (b) species of native trees found within the area (were they a factor in its selection?); (c) provisions being made to protect the longevity of the trees and its effectiveness; (d) special provisions that have been made to encourage public use of the area (are these facilities in keeping with good conservation practices?); (e) extent to which these areas are being used.

What additional areas in California would you propose to be included in any of the above categories? Discuss your proposals with as many interested people as possible. If your proposal appears to have strong general acceptance, contact the proper authorities and attempt to convince them of the merits of your proposal. As the population of California continues to grow we will need to greatly expand available and well-manned recreational facilities and especially those in which trees are a factor.

PROTECTIVE INFLUENCE OF TREES

Trees have, since early times, been used by man as a medium for protection against the adverse effect of such natural elements as heat, cold, wind, rain, and snow. Describe as many situations as you can to illustrate how trees may have been used for these purposes. The habitat of many animals is predicated on the presence of either scattered or forest trees. Name some animals that fall in this category and describe just how they are dependent on trees for food or protection or both. Trees are also an important factor in stabilizing land surfaces. Make a list, based on observation, of the various ways in which trees have been effective in this respect.

Many additional interesting and worthwhile tree activities are described by Woodbridge Metcalf in *Native Trees of the San Francisco Bay Region* (Berkeley and Los Angeles, 1959).

GLOSSARY

akene: a small, dry, hard indehiscent 1-seeded fruit.

anther: the sac or sacs containing the pollen, the essential part of the stamen.

appressed: flattened or pressed against another body but not united with it; hairs lying flat on leaves are appressed.

axillary: borne or occurring in an axil.

axils: the angle between a leaf and stem.

blade: the expanded part of a leaf or petal.

bract: the modified or much reduced leaf of a flower cluster; in Gramineae, the modified leaf subtending a spikelet; leafy bracted, in Compositae, with accessory or foliose bracts to the head outside the involucre.

calyx: the outer, usually green, whorl of the flower.

coalesced: organs of one kind that have grown together.

constricted: tightened or drawn together.

deciduous: the falling off.

dioecious: having the pistillate and the staminate flowers on different plants.

dorsal: relating to or borne along the back; lower; outer; posterior.

drupe: a fruit with a fleshy or soft outside (or exocarp) and a hard or stony inside (or endocarp).

evergreen: having leaves all year.

filaments: a thread, in case of a stamen the stalk supporting the anther.

foliose: having numerous leaves.

glabrous: bald, not hairy. Some agriculturists and some botanists wrongly use the term smooth as opposite to hairy; bald or balbrous is the opposite of hairy; smooth is the opposite of rough.

glaucous: whitened with a bloom.

globose: rounded, more or less spherical.

indehiscent: not splitting open, as an akene.

involucre: a circle of bracts enclosing a flower cluster or some fruit.

134

keel: a longitudinal central ridge on the back of an organ, like the keel of a boat; the two lower petals of a pealike flower, which are joined into a keel-like body.

key: a dried winged fruit as the fruit of maple ash or sycamore.

lanceolate: lance shaped, much longer than broad. Tapering from below the middle to the apex.

midrib: the main or central rib of a leaf.

monoecious: having the pistillate and the staminate flowers on the same plant.

naturalized: an introduced plant species that reproduces in the wild and extends its range.

obovate: inversely ovate.

ovate: like shape of a longitudinal section of a hens egg, with broad end basal.

pedicels: the stalk of a single flower in a flower cluster.

peduncle: the general term for the stalk of a flower.

petioles: the stalk of a leaf.

pinnae: leaflets or divisions of a compound leaf.

pistil: the ovule-bearing organ of a flower.

pistillate: provided with pistils and without stamens — female.

pubescent: clothed with hairs, especially soft or downy hairs.

raceme: a flower cluster in which the flowers are borne along the peduncle on pedicels of nearly equal length.

ranked: successive rows.

samara: an indehiscent winged fruit like the key of a maple.

sessile: leaf, leaf with a petiole and the blade seated directly on the stem; sessile ovary, one without a stipe.

spike: a flower cluster in which the flowers are sessile and more or less densely arranged along a common peduncle.

spurs: a slender and hollow extension or prolongation of some part of a flower, as the petal of a Columbine or calyx of a larkspur.

stamen: the male organ of a flower, which bears the pollen.

staminate: having stamens but no pistils.

stigma: the receptive part of the style which secretes a sticky or viscid substance.

stipe: the leaf stalk of a fern.

stipules: small supplementary organs or appendages of the leaf, borne in pairs at the base of the petiole.

135

stomate: a breathing pore or aperture in the epidermis.

style: the contracted or slender portion of a pistil between the ovary and stigma.

two-ranked: arranged in two vertical rows.

tomentose: covered with short, dense, soft hairs.

umbel: in a flower cluster the divisions, like the rays of an umbrella, arising from a common point.

umbellate: borne in an umbel.

ventral: relating to or borne on the face; upper; inner; anterior.

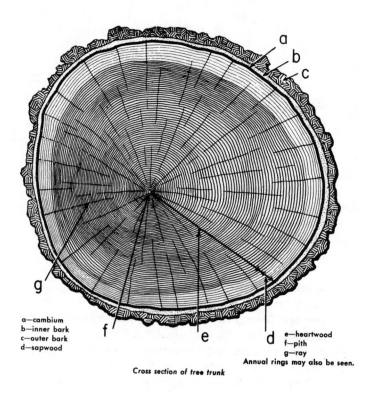

a—cambium
b—inner bark
c—outer bark
d—sapwood

e—heartwood
f—pith
g—ray
Annual rings may also be seen.

Cross section of tree trunk

Check List of Common and Scientific Names of Native or
Naturalized Trees of the Sierra Nevada

PINE FAMILY (*PINACEAE*)

One-Leaf Pinyon Pine *(Pinus monophylla)* p. 33
Lodgepole Pine *(Pinus murrayana)* p. 35, pl. 1,a
Western Yellow Pine *(Pinus ponderosa)* p. 35, pl. 1,b
Jeffrey Pine *(Pinus jeffreyi)* p. 36, pl. 1,c
Washoe Pine *(Pinus washoensis)* p. 36
Digger Pine *(Pinus sabiniana)* p. 37, pl. 1,d
Knobcone Pine *Pinus attenuata)* p. 37, pl. 2,a
Sugar Pine *(Pinus lambertiana)* p. 38, pl. 2,b
Western White Pine *(Pinus monticola)* p. 39
Bristlecone Pine *(Pinus aristata)* p. 40, pl. 2,c
Limber Pine *Pinus flexilis)* p. 40
Foxtail Pine *(Pinus balfouriana)* p. 41, pl. 2,d
Whitebark Pine *(Pinus albicaulis)* p. 42, pl. 3,a
Douglas Fir *(Pseudotsuga menziesii)* p. 42, pl. 3,b
Mountain Hemlock *(Tsuga mertensiana)* p. 43
White Fir *(Abies concolor)* p. 44, pl. 3,c
Red Fir *(Abies magnifica)* p. 45, pl. 4,a

REDWOOD FAMILY *(TAXODIACEAE)*

Giant Sequoia *(Sequoiadendron giganteum)* p. 46, pl. 4,b

CYPRESS FAMILY *(CUPRESSACEAE)*

Incense Cedar *(Calocedrus decurrens)* p. 47, pl. 4,c
MacNab Cypress *(Cupressus macnabiana)* p. 48, pl. 4,d
Piute Cypress *(Cupressus nevadensis)* p. 48
Western Juniper *(Juniperus occidentalis)* p. 49
California Juniper *(Juniperus californica)* p. 49
Utah Juniper *(Juniperus osteosperma)* p. 51, pl. 5,a

YEW FAMILY *(TAXACEAE)*

Western Yew *(Taxus brevifolia)* p. 52, pl. 5,b
California Nutmeg *(Torreya californica)* p. 52, pl. 5,c

AGAVE FAMILY *(AGAVACEAE)*

Joshua Tree *(Yucca brevifolia)* p. 53, pl. 6,a
Mojave Yucca *(Yucca schidigera)* p. 54, pl. 6,b

WILLOW FAMILY *(SALICACEAE)*

Aspen *(Populus tremuloides)* p. 57, pl. 6,c
Fremont Cottonwood *(Populus fremontii)* p. 57
Black Cottonwood *(Populus trichocarpa)* p. 58, pl. 6,d
Narrowleaf Cottonwood *(Populus angustifolia)* p. 56
Silver or White Poplar *(Populus alba)* p. 56
Lombardy Poplar *(Populus nigra* var. *italica)* p. 56
Red Willow *(Salix laevigata)* p. 59, pl. 7,a
Yellow Willow *(Salix lasiandra)* p. 59, pl. 7,b
Black Willow *(Salix gooddingii)* p. 60, pl. 7,c
Arroyo Willow *(Salix lasiolepis)* p. 60, pl. 7,d
Nuttal Willow *(Salix scouleriana)* p. 61, pl. 8,a
Sandbar Willow *(Salix hindsiana)* p. 61, pl. 8,b
Dusky Willow *(Salix melanopsis)* p. 61
MacKenzie Willow *(Salix mackenziana)* p. 62

WALNUT FAMILY *(JUGLANDACEAE)*

Hinds Black Walnut *(Juglans hindsii)* p. 63

BIRCH FAMILY *(BETULACEAE)*

Water Birch *(Betula occidentalis)* p. 64, pl. 8,c
White Alder *(Alnus rhombifolia)* p. 65
Mountain Alder *(Alnus tenuifolia)* p. 65, pl. 8,d

BEECH FAMILY *(FAGACEAE)*

Giant Chinquapin *(Castanopsis chrysophylla)* p. 67
Tanbark Oak *(Lithocarpus densiflora)* p. 67, pl. 9,a
Valley Oak *(Quercus lobata)* p. 69, pl. 9,b
Blue Oak *(Quercus douglasii)* p. 70, pl. 9,c
California Black Oak *(Quercus kelloggii)* p. 70, pl. 9,d
Canyon Live Oak *(Quercus chrysolepis)* p. 71, pl. 10,a
Interior Live Oak *(Quercus wislizenii)* p. 71, pl. 10,b
Oracle Oak *(Quercus morehus)* p. 72, pl. 10,c

LAUREL FAMILY *(LAURACEAE)*

California Laurel *(Umbellularia californica)* p. 72, pl. 10,d

SYCAMORE FAMILY *(PLATANACEAE)*

Western Sycamore *(Platanus racemosa)* p. 73

ROSE FAMILY *(ROSACEAE)*

Mountain Mahogany *(Cercocarpus ledifolius)* p. 74
Hard Tack *Cercocarpus betuloides)* p. 75, pl. 11,a
Bitter Cherry *(Prunus emarginata)* p. 76
Western Choke Cherry *(Prunus virginiana* var. *demissa)* p. 78
Sierra Plum *(Prunus subcordata)* p. 78
Toyon *(Heteromeles arbutifolia)* p. 79, pl. 11,b

QUASSIA FAMILY *(SIMURABACEAE)*

Tree of Heaven *(Ailanthus glandulosa)* p. 80

PEA FAMILY *(LEGUMINOSAE)*

Western Redbud *(Cercis occidentalis)* p. 80, pl. 11,c

CACAO FAMILY *(STERCULIACEAE)*

California Flannel Bush *(Fremontodendron californica)* p. 82

MAPLE FAMILY *(ACERACEAE)*

Mountain Maple *(Acer glabrum* var. *diffusum* and var. *torreyi)*
    p. 83
Big Leaf Maple *(Acer macrophyllum)* p. 85
Box Elder *(Acer negundo)* p. 86

BUCKTHORN FAMILY *(RHAMNACEAE)*

Cascara Sagrada *(Rhamnus purshiana)* p. 87, pl. 11,d

BUCKEYE FAMILY *(HIPPOCASTANACEAE)*

California Buckeye *(Aesculus californica)* p. 88

DOGWOOD FAMILY *(CORNACEAE)*

Mountain Dogwood *(Cornus nuttallii)* p. 89, pl. 12,a
Miners Dogwood *(Cornus sessilis)* p. 89

HEATH FAMILY *(ERICACEAE)*

Madrone *(Arbutus menziesii)* p. 90
Parry Manzanita *(Arctostaphylos manzanita)* p. 91

OLIVE FAMILY *(OLEACEAE)*

Flowering Ash *(Fraxinus dipetala)* p. 93
Arizona Ash *(Fraxinus velutina* var. *coriacea)* p. 93
Dwarf Ash *(Fraxinus anomala)* p. 95, pl. 12,b
Oregon Ash *(Fraxinus latifolia)* p. 96, pl. 12,c

HONEYSUCKLE FAMILY *(CAPRIFOLIACEAE)*

Blue Elderberry *(Sambucus caerulea)* p. 97, pl. 12,d

SUGGESTED REFERENCES

Abrams, Leroy. *Illustrated Flora of the Pacific States.* Stanford
Press. Vol. I, II, III, 1955; Vol. IV, Roxanna S. Ferris, 1959.

Griffin, James R., and Critchfield, William B. *The Distribution of
Forest Trees in California.* U.S.D.A. Forest Service Research
Paper PSW-82 1972.

Jaeger, Edmund C., and Arthur C. Smith. *Introduction to the
Natural History of Southern California.* Berkeley and Los
Angeles: University of California Press, 1966.

Munz, Philip, and David D. Keck. *California Flora and Supplement.*
Berkeley and Los Angeles: University of California Press,
1973.

McMinn, Howard E., and Evelyn Maino. *An illustrated Manual of
California Trees.* Berkeley and Los Angeles: University of
California Press, 1963

Sudworth, George B. *Forest Trees of the Pacific Slope.* New
York: Dover, 1967.

Jepson, Willis Lynn. *Trees of California.* Berkeley Associated
Students Store, 1923.

Jepson, Willis Lynn. *A Manual of the Flowering Plants of California.* Berkeley and Los Angeles: University of California
Press, reprinted 1966.

Ornduff, Robert. *Introduction to California Plant Life.* Berkeley
and Los Angeles, University of California Press, 1974.

Smith, Arthur C. *Introduction to the Natural History of the San
Francisco Bay Region.* Berkeley and Los Angeles: University of California Press, 1959.

Peattie, Donald C. *A Natural History of Western Trees.* Boston:
Houghton Mifflin, 1953.

Peterson, P. Victor. *Native Trees of Southern California.* Berkeley and Los Angeles: University of California Press, 1966.

Metcalf, Woodbridge W. *Native Trees of the San Francisco Bay
Region.* Berkeley and Los Angeles: University of California Press, 1959.

Watts, Tom. *California Tree Finder.* Berkeley Nature Study
Guild, P. O. Box 972, Berkeley, California 1963.

INDEX